Go Splash!!
Waves of Aloha

Kevin England DC. DD.

Grosvenor House
Publishing Limited

All rights reserved
Copyright © Kevin England, 2023

The right of Kevin England to be identified as the author of this
work has been asserted in accordance with Section 78
of the Copyright, Designs and Patents Act 1988

The book cover is copyright to Kevin England

This book is published by
Grosvenor House Publishing Ltd
Link House
140 The Broadway, Tolworth, Surrey, KT6 7HT.
www.grosvenorhousepublishing.co.uk

This book is sold subject to the conditions that it shall not, by way of
trade or otherwise, be lent, resold, hired out or otherwise circulated
without the author's or publisher's prior consent in any form of
binding or cover other than that in which it is published and
without a similar condition including this condition being
imposed on the subsequent purchaser.

This book is a work of fiction. Any resemblance to
people or events, past or present, is purely coincidental.

A CIP record for this book
is available from the British Library

ISBN 978-1-80381-680-7

Preface:

Although I didn't know it at the time, looking back I was first introduced to the surf therapy concept in Australia in '84 by a Vietnam vet, who was using surfing to free his mind.

We met on a beach in Queensland, one of us was surfin' the concentrated energy waves of the body, and the other was riding the liquid energy waves of the Ocean. This amazing Vietnam survivor was using surfing to 'free his mind' after the horrors of the war, while I was on the beach teaching a free liberated form of 'wave massage' which he referred to as a different kinda 'Bodysurfin' – one that brought him a great sense of peace, and when fused together with his ocean surfing, created a kinda magic.

We spent every minute together for six weeks, he would be either surfing the ocean waves, having a 'wave' massage, or sharing this philosophy on life. This special moment in time was the basis of our 'living aloha' concept.

My first experience of the beach and the joy it could bring started many years before this Australian encounter but forget rose-tinted glasses for many Londoners growing up as a kid meant playing on bomb sites, London was bleak, the city was covered in a blanket of coal smog and the buildings looked filthy and black.

A few bright lights shone through the gloom and for me it was Tower Beach in the City of London. Where twice a day, the river Thames swells with tidal water, washing the ancient embankments and tossing up centuries of junk onto the foreshore, feeding the greatest hobby for any Cockney kid, Mudlarking.

Mudlarking is a kind of dirty beach combing, but the shells we would find are more likely to come from an ancient musket or a World War II bomb case. Coins, bits of pottery and medieval clay pipes adorned our collections. Animal bones, broken glass, and sewage were left to be washed away by the incoming tide, then replaced with more treasure on its next ebb and flow.

My beach was also full of awe and wonder and I loved it........

"We know instinctively that being near water makes us healthier and happier, reduces stress, and brings us peace" -W.J. Nichols-Blue Mind

Introduction:

The aim of this book is to help us engage in mindful activities, creating a state of mind that embraces positive mental health and wellbeing.

We will show you how to think differently about life's inevitable struggles, and provide a few tricks and tips, to surf the waves of emotion that we face every day.

The biggest difference between peace and stress is attitude, and the best strategy for living is to make the greatest use of the present moment.

The key is to realize that the vast majority of worries, frustrations, disappointments, and stressful thoughts we deal with, are a product of our own creation, you are what you think.

Mind waves (your thought waves) determine the quality of your life, we will show you how to select a better wave to ride, one that improves your life's quality.

The best way to use this book is to first read cover to cover. Then just open randomly when you feel the need for inspiration, or simply choose a story that fits your mood.

Completing the interactive section at the end of the book, will help you consolidate your understanding.

If you take away and surf just one wave (inspired idea) from this book, then its mission accomplished.

If this book helps you in any way, please share the aloha, pay forward, give a copy as a gift to someone who you think would also benefit from its story, and start to create your own magic.

This book is for anyone with an open mind and a loving heart, people who are not afraid to embrace the child within, smile, laugh and be happy. The focus of this book is aimed at those who wish to bring about change, build a brighter future, create good vibrations, and have the ride of their lives.

Mindful activities can lead to good vibrations, focus on riding that energy wave and you will become emersed in magic moments. These occur when you change the way someone feels, for the better, including yourself.

Choose your Wave..........

Happy Surfing.........

CONTENTS:

Preface:	iii
Introduction:	v
Contents:	vii
Prologue:	ix
Rolling:	1
The Cave:	10
Wayfinding:	14
Bubbles:	19
Balance:	21
Flip-it:	24
Wipeout:	27
Splash:	31
Starfish:	33
Mino:	35
Pebble:	37
Squishy:	39
Lia Tree:	42
Hoppi:	45
Happy Days:	48
Waters of Life:	51

Finding Focus:	54
Fun of Focus:	57
Moments:	60
Waves of Aloha:	63
The Key:	67
Pele:	79
Note from Mojo:	86
Go Splash (interactive section):	88
Afterword:	113
Oceanic Heritage:	115
About the Author:	116
Living Aloha:	118
Bibliography:	120

In Polynesia, where surfing began.....................

The relationship with the waves, movement and power of the ocean is used to reflect the relationship with mind waves, body movement, and a person's soul. For we live our lives on an ocean of emotion and are washed with waves of thoughts and feelings every moment of everyday.

You can't stop the waves, but you can learn to surf........

"You can't always change your circumstances, but you can always change your attitude about your circumstances. The problem, then, isn't the problem. The problem is the way you are thinking about it." -Michelle Obama

A wave is liquid, fast moving and full of energy, therefore a waverider should adopt a liquidity of body, elasticity of mind, and embrace their own spirited entity.

"Open your Blue Mind and the ports of call will become visible." -W. J. Nichols

Come and experience Mojos adventure as he is first hit by waves of hardship, hopelessness, and depression. As he learns to see the unseen, to hear the unheard, and to know the unknown. Stay with him as he gains the knowledge to choose his own wave and develops the skills to surf upon waves of joy, fun and happiness.

Feel safe knowing that you too can:

Go Splash, be joyful, have fun, and be kind.

Rolling:

Mojo was rollin' down the hill with his best friend Billy perched on the back of his skateboard, when all of a sudden, the Banga Boys jumped out from behind a bush knocking him into the gutter. "I want your board" said arch-rival Biffa. "But it's my birthday present" protested Mojo.

"Aha diddum's" said Biffa, "Boo Hoo, I'll tell you what, just to make it fair I'm going to toss you for it" he put his hand into his pocket and fondled his two headed coin. He had won many a bet with this coin and all the local kids knew about it. However, Mojo was too afraid to say no, he just wanted to get away, so he had a quick look around and said, "Okay, but your mate Sidelight gets to call heads or tails" laughing aloud all the Banga Boys agreed.

Now Sidelight was a young car mechanic who got his nickname because he was not bright enough to be a headlight.

Biffa flipped the coin in the air, it turned once, then twice, it hovered a little and descended towards the tarmac, as it hit the road Sidelight shouted "tails." Then there was a long silence, the gang where startled, stupid Sidelight had called tails on a two headed coin, why? Soon, Biffa and the gang started shouting, pushing, and berating him, in the confusion Mojo grabbed Billy, jumped onto his skateboard, and shot-off down the hill as fast as he could towards the small harbour at the edge of the town, realising that they had been duped the gang stopped arguing and chased after Mojo while still shouting abuse at Sidelight.

Bumpety bump, went the board over the cobbles of the harbour, bump, bump, bump, went the wheels on the wooden pier "get the rope" said Mojo has he jumped from the skateboard onto his little boat, Billy followed with the frayed rope in his mouth. "Come on. Come on" said Mojo as he frantically tried to start the engine, the Banga Boys were now running along the rickety pier which was shaking with each step, one more pull thought Mojo, Burr! Burr! The engine came to life and the boat pulled away from its anchorage, just as the Banga Boys arrived "I'll kill you" shouted Biffa as he watched Mojo and Billy disappear around the end of the pier, the wild wind hit his face and lifted his hair as they left the harbour with a smile and a shaka.

"We had better go and stay with auntie" said Mojo "we will wait a few days until things cool down" Billy nodded and smiled; he liked auntie she always gave him plenty of treats and lets him play with the chickens. Mojo had done the journey many times, but never by himself, Papa had always driven the boat. Okay thought Mojo to himself, we make our way outside the reef and turn left, then it's across the strait, continue between the twin islands and the head north for eight hours. Mojo also liked auntie, she lived on a beautiful green island and spent most of her day attending to the plants and animals on her smallholding, in the evening they would sit around the campfire and listen as she played on her ukulele and sang sweet melodies, Mojo would lay on the grass and look at the billions of stars twinkling in the night sky. Mojo loved the bigness and wildness of the sea, along with its constantly changing moods. He sat back into the boat and started thinking about auntie, the last time he saw

GO SPLASH!!

her she put on the D--n-y film Moana and said "you see this girl, she is your ancestor, she did great things in her life, and if you copy her you will also do great things, for you have the same brilliance in your blood" auntie was always letting her imagination go, she truly is a free spirit thought Mojo as he drifted into a deep sleep beneath a sea of stars.

Mojo was a typical pacific island twelve-year-old he wore T-shirts and boardshorts, he wore his cap backwards, liked skateboarding, and was into island vibe music and street dancing. He was funny and very popular with the other Keiki (children), and he went everywhere with his best friend Billy. Everyone loved Billy his white coat was splattered in brown and black patches in fact he look more like a Dalmatian in colour than a little goat. They looked the picture of contentment wrapped around each other, sharing the warmth of their bodies under the moonlight.

Mojo woke startle, he was wet, it was raining, the sky was dark, a storm was blowing in and the waves were blowing up, a Kraken appeared to be rising from the dark depths. As the waves got higher and higher, the sea became angry, Mojo became frightened, he was worried about falling overboard, so he used the frayed rope to tie both Billy and himself to the boat. Thunder and lightning danced through the sky, and the large dark waves looking like monsters from the deep which shook his soul, the boat flipped then righted itself, Mojo and Billy were in the water secured only by a thread, a worn lifeline of fabric, inch by inch they pulled themselves though the water and back onto that little wooden boat. This scene was repeated again and again throughout the night, as Mojo and Billy got weaker and weaker the tempest got stronger and stronger smashing the boat with all its might. "Hold on Billy, hold on" shouted Mojo against the deafening sound of the roaring beast.

With the huge waves exploding around them, they held each other and prayed, the first wave took them up into the dark angry sky and the second wave pounded down with all its might, then with a loud crack, it broke the back of the boat, it smashed the craft and pushed its occupants towards the ocean floor, they were under the water for one minute, then two or was it three, time stood still as Mojo struggled trying not to pass out. The fear barrelled in like a rogue wave and the feeling overwhelmed Mojo, is this the end thought the scared boy, he passed out with the voice of this Hawaiian hero Eddie Aikau in his head.

"When you are on the edge of the abyss you see things as they truly are, nothing matters, all your worries, all your fears are not important, the most important thing is getting that one tiny breath of air, to be re-born, to be given a new day.

Only when you are fully in the moment, fully committed, at that precious moment in time, when anything you thought was impossible becomes possible, only then will you feel fully alive."

Mojo slowly open his eyes, Billy was licking his face, they were still attached by strands of a tattered rope, and at the other end there was a single plank half buried in the soft sand, white foam bubbled around them, they were on a beach, but where? Feeling the warmth of the sun on his face, Mojo had a little chuckle as he remembered auntie once saying "no matter how strong the waves, or how bad the storm, it will eventually pass, and the sun will shine again" with tears in his eyes he began to smile, then laugh, the relief, he had faced his worst fear and survived.

Tired and hungry Mojo and Billy looked around the crescent shaped bay, he could see a reef running along the horizon and assumed that was the reason that the boat smash on impact. The beach consisted of soft white sand and a few broken pieces of coral, dense vegetation and tall slender coconut palm trees were everywhere. Tropical birds waded in the swallows of the lagoon, twisted driftwood peppered the beach, looking like they had never been touched, and beyond the green wall he could see an old volcano.

Hundreds of fish were reflected in the clear blue water of the lagoon, coconuts lay along the edge of the shoreline and there was plenty of brushwood to make a fire, this is good thought Mojo as he set about collecting sticks for the fire and food for a meal, today he was going to celebrate just being alive.

Full of gratitude, rested and with a belly full of food, Mojo made a commitment to climb up the side of the volcanic hill in the morning, he would go as high as he could to get a view of the island, but for now he was just going to explore the rock pools to the left of the beach which seemed to be teeming with life.

Billy found a flat rock just under the water's surface to stand on, this kept him cool in the hot sun, from here he watched Mojo dipping in and out of the water while playing with the fish and crabs, that looks like fun thought Billy, "Ouch!" said Mojo as he stubbed his toe on something sharp hidden under the flat rock that Billy was standing on. Mojo took a deep breath, put his head under the water and had a quick look hoping to see the offending object, he saw small rocks and broken shells but quickly identified a conch shell buried in the sand. Mojo had a bright idea for the use of the conch, and he spent the rest of the afternoon trying to free the shell, but it was well and truly wedged between the flat rock and the sand bed, I'll try that again later thought Mojo as the sun started to go down but for now I need to make a bed.

The next few days flew pass as Mojo and Billy explored much of the island, and from an advantage point near the top of the redundant volcano, Mojo could see that the island was uninhabited, but there were signs of a previous occupation, he could see stone platforms that had been used to build huts upon, before being abandoned and reclaimed by nature. He found taro still growing in what was once cultivate ground and a freshwater spring nearby, there were feral chickens that had made their home in the ruins, this is great thought Mojo, we have food and fresh eggs, I wonder who these people were? thought Mojo as he observed the sights. He then turned his mind back onto his present predicament, "when we get back I'm going to try and remove the conch shell from under the flat stone, it will make a great horn to alert any passing ship" he said to Billy.

Mojo had gathered five scalloped shells for digging, and a piece of driftwood for leverage along with a small rock. Armed with his new tools and a load of enthusiasm Mojo and Billy made their way over to the rock pool, the tide had just gone out which gave them time to complete the task of freeing the conch shell from its bed of sand.

Working away, and using the scalloped shells as shovels, Mojo was able to remove much of the loose soft sand at the bottom of the pool and from around and underneath the conch shell, but despite all the challenging work it was still stuck solid against the flat stone. Then he had an idea, he placed the narrow end of the driftwood into the small gap under the shell and then pushed the small rock against the driftwood he now could use the rock as a fulcrum and the wood as a lever, pushing hard on the large end of the driftwood Mojo hoped to unjam the shell, but after several attempts and no movement, he gave up on the idea, and instead turned his attention to the flat rock above the shell, I wonder if I could lever the flat rock up a little he thought.

Mojo moved the driftwood, and this time placed it under the flat rock which he then tried to lever, even Billy joined in by bouncing on the end of the driftwood, this gave Mojo yet another idea, if he stood on the high large rock above the flat one and jumped onto the end of the driftwood he might just get enough leverage to move it.

After a few moments, everything was in place and now was the decisive moment, standing about two meters above the driftwood and holding a heavy rock in order to increase his weight Mojo jumped.

Crack... Splash... Ouch... the driftwood had broken, and Mojo was lying in the rock pool nursing a bruised leg and a sprained foot from the heavy rock. "You idiot!" Mojo shouted aloud, so that all could hear. A small part of the flat rock had come away and was standing upright in the rock pool, he once again moved the now broken driftwood behind the flat rock and pulled down, the small broken part of the flat rock moved again, it then fell onto the bottom of the rock pool Mojo could now free the conch shell. Dipping his head under the water and working with the scalloped shells Mojo eased the Conch away from its resting place. He sat up in the water with the shell in his hands, Billy was bouncing with excitement, then he saw it! Light was coming from a small cave inside the large lava rock and shining through the water where the conch had been. I'm going to explore that cave tomorrow when the tide is low again thought Mojo, but tonight I'm going to clean my prize conch.

They both sat warming themselves by the fire, that Mojo had made from dried seaweed and broken twigs, they looked in awe at the gleaming shell, several hours had pasted, gone in a flash while cleaning the conch, it had been coated in algae and had been full of wet sand. There looks like a small hole in the back thought Mojo, I wonder if I can produce a sound, he took a deep breath and blow into the conch, the last few grains of sand took flight and fell onto the beach, and then he heard a whisper "I am the Shell of Sounds, I am called Echo" said a soft voice, "what" exclaimed Mojo "I am the Shell of Sounds, and I live in the cave" replied the voice. Is the shell really talking to me or is the whispering sound just the sea pulsating from inside the shell thought Mojo. Then he heard it again "I am the Shell of Sounds; I live in the cave, and I am called Echo."

He dropped the shell and backed away to the tree line.

Mojo felt uneasy he lived in a modern world and was a teenager educated in the best school on the island, he knew that shells can't talk. But he was also aware of another possibility, his auntie had always shared stories of spirits, magic, and ancestral myths. He knew about the frightening stories of the Night Marchers, and Pele the goddess of the volcano, he was scared, what had he found? Determined not to make his plight any worse, Mojo vailed to take the shell back to the cave where he had found it.

As soon as the water was low enough Mojo dived under the remaining section of flat rock and started to remove the compacted sand bed, the entrance to the cave was small, Mojo was hoping to make the hole big enough for him to get into the cave entrance and replace the shell to its rightful home.

After several hours of digging all that stood between Mojo and the entrance to the cave was floating seaweed. "If I pull the seaweed away from around the entrance just under the flat rock I might be able to just squeeze through the gap and into the cave," said Mojo sharing his thoughts with Billy.

Mojo popped his head up inside the cave and was immediately captivated by the sight. The sunlight was streaming through holes in the lava walls and reflecting on crystals inside the cave which then in-turn radiated back various shades of colours, hues of light twisting and turning, creating a wonderous dance moving in tune with the gentle sway of the waves.

After several minutes of just staring at this unexpected and magical light show, Mojo bent down into the water and with his outstretched hand he felt around for the conch shell, took hold, and pulled it up through the hole, he placed it onto what looked like a stone shelf right next to a small puddle and climbed up behind it. "There you are Echo" said Mojo. A soft voice echoed around the cave "Mahalo" (thank you). Startled! Mojo simply replied, "your welcome."

What followed in the next few moments shocked Mojo to the core.

The soft whisper coming from Echo started to explain that this island was called Motunui and was the childhood home of Moana. Each evening at sunset when the tide was low she would swim under the flat rock and come into the cave, then she would share with Echo her days experiences and all the things she had learnt, "the vibration of her words are etched into my very being, recorded forever in my inner chamber, I am the diary of her school years, listen carefully and you will hear her voice".

Placing the shell against his ear Mojo heard the voice of Moana "Today I found a cave......"

The Cave:

Moana was sitting on the sand with her best friend, a little pig called Pua, she was angry, frustrated, and upset with her father, he had just denied her request to go sailing, simply saying "it's too dangerous and you're too young" "it's not fair" said Moana stamping her feet in frustration, as she lifted her foot she noticed Crusty running sideways towards them "come on you two, let's play" said Crusty.

'Plop' Moana heard the sound of Crusty falling into the rock pool as he tried to hide from her, "3-2-1 I'm coming" said Moana, it was her turn to seek Crusty's hiding place. She looked into the clear water of the small rock pool, it was teaming with life and there were quite a few hiding places, but there was no sign of the old crab, she carefully stepped into the deeper part of the pool, and she used her thin polished oyster shell as a looking glass. Colourful fish swan around her feet their tails zigging and zagging as they moved, others stayed motionless against the shady side of the rocks.

But where was Crusty? To her left Moana noticed a small cloud of sand just under the flat rock, she dipped her head into the clear water, knelt down and looked under the flat rock, there was no sign of Crusty, but she could see a stream of bright light shining from under the rock, she often sat on the flat rock as she marvelled at the fish swimming all around her feet, the shallowness transforms the water into a magnifying glass. There's often more to see below the surface than above, it was her own private aquarium, shared only with her ocean friends.

After taking a big gulp of air Moana dove headfirst under the flat rock and directly into the stream of light, the gap was small but just big enough for a little girl to squeeze through, one stroke, then another, the light was getter brighter, just one more stroke, then......

Moana found herself inside a small compact black lava cave, there was sunlight shining through peppered holes in encrusted casing of the rock creating streams of dancing light as it bounced off the water's surface and illuminated the glittering walls of the cave.

"Wow!" Said Moana "I've played in this rock pool all my life and didn't even know that this cave was here."

"This cave is a home for the mystic, a portal between what is and what can be, the energy found in the space between thought and perception is known as the azura" said Crusty "azura is the spirit of change and transformation; one that changes imagination into action and action into reality, a wave of pure potential."

"Wow!" Said Moana as she noticed a puddle or was it another pool within the cave, its crystal blue waters looked, enchanting. "That" said Crusty "is a magic pool, a window into a world where anything is possible, come let me show you."

"You can do anything, you can learn anything, and you can be anything, what would you like to do?" said Crusty, "I want to learn to sail, to take one of the big canoes beyond the reef, can I do that?" said Moana, "Yes just ask azura to show you" no sooner than Moana placed the request with azura that things started to happen, the blue water turned into a screen, on the screen was a teenaged Moana standing on a large outrigger canoe holding the rope leading to a big red sail, the canoe was cutting through the waves, this was exciting thought Moana. Soon the image could be seen on all the walls of the cave, all around was water, the floor was moving she was on the canoe, really on the canoe, she was sailing! The wind was in her hair, and sea spray on her face, she could feel the power of the sail pulling on her arms, this is fun thought Moana, real fun.

Right then, at the moment of sheer joy she heard a voice, a gentle voice in her head 'Moana we live our lives on an Ocean of emotion, every minute of every day, we experience waves of thoughts and feelings, some high, some low, the peaks and troths will come and go, sometimes the water will be calm and other times there will be storms. Storms so bad, so rough that you will fear that you might not survive, you can't stop the waves, but you can learn to sail and surf the waves, waves are energy and just like thoughts and feelings, you can choose to ride them or just let them go. So go splash, go play, have fun, and develop the skills of wave riding from inside the reef, it's a safe zone, and when you are a little older and ready you will go sailing, just like you have been shown today, and remember, after every storm the sun always shines. No matter how upset you are, things will always get better.'

"Moana" said crusty "I can hear the call of the conch from the village telling us that the tide is turning, we need to go" as he finished his words the vision of their virtual reality experience disappeared and Moana found herself on the floor of the cave, smiling, wet, but happy.

"Can I come again" said Moana, "the cave is accessible twice a day at low tide, but the azura will only be present at dawn or dusk as she lives in the space of transformation betwixt and between what is and what can be, visit then and explore more possibilities, just as Lava flow created this cave, mindflow creates your thoughts, feelings and emotions, she can show you how to ride those waves".

"Before we go Crusty I must save this experience" said Moana, she picked up a large conch shell and started talking into its heart.

"Today I found a cave...."

Wayfinding:

Mojo looked deep into the dark blue pool and asked the azura "I've just heard Moana talk about learning to sail a canoe, in her D--n-y film the demigod Maui, taught her the art of wayfinding by using his hand and the stars, was that even possible?"

Above the cave the morning sun burns the sky clear of clouds, but within the cave things changed, the smooth water in the pool was now textured by raindrops, the lights having dimmed, a beautiful rainbow uncurled itself from the pool, filling the cave with ore and wonder, it then shot up through the roof to embrace the heavens. Mojo was sitting on an imagined canoe as it dutifully followed the fluttering rainbow, he drifted with the wind through the gateway to the great salty wilderness and found himself afloat in a timeless strange land on a delightful moonlit night, stars were glimmering through the gaps of shimmering colours.

Wayfinding is a bridge to the pass. It's a tradition that goes back thousands of years of trying to understand the ocean, it's a huge bank of knowledge that's passed on from generation to generation.

Polynesian culture centres around the ocean, today's Polynesians are world renowned for surfing, but few of them ever sail. That was not always the way, they were the greatest water people on earth, living on the ocean in the most dynamic mood changing and unforgiving environment known to man. They could decipher clues from the waves, the stars, and the oceans creatures, they sailed the Pacific by learning from it, and joyfully accepting its mysteries. The essence of being a wayfinder is having the knowledge and confidence to live and do anything you want on the ocean.

"We are going to navigate the old way; we are going to follow the stars at night, the rise and fall of the sun during the day, we will also watch the swells, currents and sea birds" said an apparition that looked like Maui. "If you go to sea without a guide, you may take many weeks, to do a two-day journey. The canoe was the spaceship of your ancestors, they were explorers sailing thousands of miles into unknown territory using the stars as guides. The maps to new lands were found in the skies, they were guided by a compass of stars shining in the heavens."

Mojo held tight and listened intently as Maui proceeded sharing knowledge and giving advice, while also loving the sound of his own voice.

"Learning should be something very special, very exciting, the ocean is my classroom, here you can learn the art of wayfinding and celestial navigation. To many the ocean is a desert with its dune like swells. But with intimate understanding of the night sky, you can map a course by knowing where certain stars rise and set each night on the horizon, plan your route, and follow your plan." Maui was smiling the biggest smile; he was having fun and saw himself as some sort of (Kahuna) an expert wayfinder, tattoos on his arms clapped in unison as though applauding a great wisdom keeper.

"In natures classroom, he continued, we are permitted to remain children all our lives. There is always something new to comprehend, beyond facts, labels, charts, things you can only see with the mind's eye."

To truly appreciate this sacred knowledge, you've got to go back to the source, the moon and stars can help us understand our moods. A complex design of graphic communication tattooed on his body, moved as a visual display of the story being told.

'I gazed up at the stars. So far from light pollution, they were stunning. The Milky Way stretched diagonally across the sky. The longer I looked, the more stars I saw, until it seemed as if the entire sky was glittering with diamonds. As I lay there on my little boat, I imagined the planets and moons orbiting all the stars, and for a precious moment I forgot everything. I simply allowed myself to be absorbed into the spellbinding beauty of the night sky. For a brief, incredible moment, I transcended my puny existence, feeling as tiny and insignificant as a mote of dust, but at the same time at one with the infinite majesty of the universe. I was everything, and everything was me. I was everywhere, and nowhere, I knew everything, and I knew nothing. I was eternal, and I was intensely present.' -Roz Savage

The two great lights that shine on the earth, the sun, and the moon, affect all that happens on the land and in the waters of our world.

The energy from our nearest star, the sun, provides life on earth by way of heat and light. The light from the sun not only provides day and night but also seasonal influences on our systems, which in turn bring about physiological and emotional changes.

The moon affects the life cycle and behaviour of many different animals, it influences the stability of the earth's rotation around the sun, its gravitational pull is so powerful it creates the great movement of the tides, and as our bodies consist of much water, we too respond to this tidal effect.

When the moon is full, it can bring all of our emotions to the surface and amplify them, this is not necessary a terrible thing as it's only when our feelings rise up, that they can move out of us. Conversely new moons create more calm and reflective periods.

'Ocean eddies can be real buggers because there are so many variables at play in the ocean, not just winds at the surface, but also salinity, water density, the pull of the moon, the Earth's rotation, islands and land mases and topography of the ocean floor. Unlike winds that let us know by their touch on our skin how strong they are and where they are ging, eddies lurk unseen and unseeable. A seafarer can't detect an eddy until they are in it, and they notice their boat is spinning around in circles and is no longer going where they want it to go.' -Roz Savage

People are much like stars, they shine with light, give warmth, and burn with inner fire. They are energy, cosmic energy, and we need to learn, to surf that cosmic wave.

Go with the flow, be like water, remain fluid, make subtle adjustments, tune-into the eternal rhythm, start enjoying the ebb and flow of being alive. When we navigate life this way, we liberate the mind and pacify the soul, finding our own wave, for ourselves.

'Live as water, you are water and water is you. You spent the first nine months of life floating in and being nourished by amniotic fluid, (which is 98% water) and truly unconditional love flowing into you, flowing as you. There is a mysterious magical nature to this liquid energy that we often take for granted. Try to squeeze it, and it eludes us; relax our hands into it, and we experience it readily. If it stays stationary, it becomes stagnant; if it is allowed to flow, it will stay pure. It does not seek the high spots to be above it all but settles for the lowest places. It gathers into rivers, lakes, and streams; courses to the sea; and then evaporates to fall again as rain. It maps out nothing and it plays no favourites: It doesn't intend to provide sustenance to the animals and plants. It has no plans to irrigate the fields; to slake our thirst; or to provide the opportunity to swim, ski, surf, fish, scuba dive, or drink. These are some of the benefits that come naturally from water simply doing what it does and being what it is, not trying to do anything other than simply flow. As you can see there are parallels between you and this naturally flowing substance that allows life to sustain itself. Live as water lives since you are water, and you will nourish others without trying.' – Wayne W. Dyer.

Sailing the seas of the mind requires navigating skills and knowledge gained by the practice of wayfinding. When you develop your own ability to sail the ocean in front of you, you learn how to think, feel, and see for yourself, you transform outer guidance into inner guidance.

The more we learn, the more we realize how little we truly understand, thought Mojo.

Many ocean miles had passed under the hull of the canoe, it felt like he have been out for hours trapped in some kind of time warp, then a hailstorm hit, waves splashed onto the canoe, the hailstones pinging painfully off Mojo's ears, nose and hands bringing him instantly back into reality, he was lying on the cave floor wet and cold, the tide had turned, and the sea was rising, it was time to leave.

Bubbles:

"Today I met Bubbles in the rock pool just outside this cave, she is a funny little rainbow fish ablaze with a coat of wonderful colours, she just loves blowing bubbles, playing with crabs and all the other fish, especially those left in the rock pool long after the tide had returned to the ocean. Some of the bubbles are just so beautiful and they seem to last forever. Let me tell you something about little Bubbles" said Moana as she spoke into the shell of sounds, recording forever the story of her new friend.

"Bubbles will lose most of her memory when she falls asleep making each day a new experience. But she does have a unique gift, she has the ability to store happy memories in protective bubbles, the type that can float in the water and last for a very long time.

When she sees something that makes her laugh, smile, or feel happy, she will create an image in her mind, and then encases it in a transparent bubble. The bubble will float protected under the water; happy memories stored for a later date. Then one day, long after she had forgotten all about what happened. She can look at the picture captured within the bubble and see the image that made her feel happy, when she sees the image, she will experience the same happy feeling that she had when creating the bubble. It's her way of preserving memories."

After listening to the story, Mojo though that he could do something similar to make himself be happy and feel good.

When I get back home I'm going to take photos of things that make me happy, that make me laugh. Then when I'm feeling a bit down I can look at the photos and feel happy, I might even do this with music and create a happy music playlist.

Brilliant idea thought Mojo.

Just brilliant.....

"Bubbles up; They will point you towards home, no matter how deep or how far you roam. Just know that you are loved, there is light up above, and the joy is always enough.......Bubbles up" – Jimmy Buffett.

Bubbles up; is confirmation that the feeling of love, joy, and aloha, is flowing and everything is okay, no matter how bad the situation.

Balance:

Self-conquest is the greatest of victories. -Plato

"Today I learnt to Surf, well nearly" was Moana's opening line.

"Let's get started, one day Maui cut the Alaia board out of the Willwilli tree and taught a man to surf, to overcome his fears. So, from the beginning surfing was the art of overcoming one's fears, if you want to learn how to surf you have to master the art of Pono (balance) and learning any art requires practice, lots and lots of practice." Said Keli her surf instructor. Moana and her two friends were told to lay on the surfboard and paddle out a short distance into the lagoon, this morning the water looked magnificent while reflecting different shades of jade and blue, slowly one hand after another they paddled as instructed "okay, stop. Just float a while in the calm water, relax, feel the gentle waves rolling under the board, feel the rhythm, feel the pulse, and notice how good you feel, that's because you have balance" they all looked at each other and giggled, this was fun.

"Now sit up, put your legs over each side of the board and stay balanced, make sure that you are sitting on the centre line" there was a little rocking, but they all managed to sit up on the board. "Now" said Keli, "when you are ready I want you to stand up, remember stay on the middle line of the board and keep your balance."

Slowly they raised up onto their feet, then splash! One fell in, then another, before long all three were in the warm water, splashing, laughing, and having fun.

After a while Keli told the Keiki (children) to get back onto their boards and he then asked them, why did they fall off the board, because we lost balance they all shouted, "correct" said Keli. "Remember this; you are either in balance (Pono) or you are not in balance, if you do the right things (pono) you will be in balance, it is black and white, it's one thing or the other, there is no in-between. You are either on your board or you're in the water, un-balance in the wai" (water).

"It's the same with life, you are either in control, in balance, riding the waves of thoughts, feelings and emotions, or you're in the surf, emersed in emotions, unable to control your thoughts or feelings, tumbling around in the rough water, getting hurt and taking hit after hit, wave after wave. The key to balance is to control your emotions, you choose your wave, (how you wish to feel) and keep moving forward, and yet accept that sometimes you will have to shift sideways or even turn around to maintain momentum.

For the rest of the day all three played on their boards, lying, sitting, and standing, trying to learn to balance as the gentle waves rolled under, they constantly fell into to the water as they practiced, but safe in the knowledge that the water in the lagoon was shallow, warm, and calm, all day they slowly practiced the art of staying in Pono.

Moana would remember Keli's words spoken on that day for the rest of her life "do you control your emotions or do your emotions control you? Are you in Pono or not in pono? Are you on the board or in the water? You can't stop the waves, but you can learn to sail and surf, and it all starts with balance and balance starts with practice, little by little you will learn the first steps of wave riding."

"You go out surfing to ride the waves, it's like a dance, a communication between yourself and the ocean. The object is to achieve harmony with the manifestation of nature"
- Eddie Aikau

Mojo recognised the wisdom in the words. You can't control what happens to you, like being shipwrecked on this island, but you can control how you respond, by changing the way of how you look at things and how you think about things, you can change the way you feel, he let the thought drift away as he took in the last glowing rays of a beautiful sunset. He was now busy gathering apples from the cactus bushes and shellfish which grew on the rocks along the shore. Mojo collected them at low tide in a bucket made from a coconut hask, he removed the flesh from the shell and placed it on flat rocks to dry out Billy would stand on guard protecting the supper from the gaze of the hungry sea birds.

"I saw him smiling in what felt like the first time in two years, standing on a board surfing towards me, I don't think he's felt pure joy in all that time. The world inside his head is a pretty dark place, this got him back into simple reality. It's priceless." -the Joy of Surf Therapy

Flip-it:

"Today I learnt what to do if I was knocked off the canoe or dumped off my surfboard and fell into deep water." Said Echo as it recited the next recorded page of Moana's diary.

Mojo pressed Echo closer to his ear having just been shipwrecked he thought that this might be a useful thing to hear.

"After teaching us about balance Keli showed us how to recover if we fell from our boards into the water. Often when we surface following a wipeout our surfboard will be upside down with the fin sticking up into the air, when this happens you need to grab hold of the board, gather your breath and composure, then 'flip' the board over before pulling yourself back on top. If the board is too big or the task is to hard then don't be afraid to ask for help, if the canoe is upside down then it may take many hands to 'flip' it back into the right position, before you can climb back onboard and recover from the wipeout."

Keli said, "it's the same with any problem in life, if you are in deep water or in deep trouble your view of the issue is often upside down, very negative and disheartening, to find a way back onboard you have to be able to see the other side, and you can only do that by 'flipping' it over. If your view of the problem is negative then 'flip' it over and look at the positive side. Scream if you have to, it's an intense pressure release valve, then compose yourself 'it is what it is' then ask yourself, is there another way of looking at this and what options do I have, then act, this is 'flipping' in process.

Flip for fun, is a great practice of looking for the funny side, the good side, the bright side, the positive side of the situation, and will often affect the outcome, as it changes your actions and your feelings, and as a bonus it will make for a happier life.

When you wake up each day, you should be filled with excitement because you know the day is going to be full of wonderful things. You are meant to be laughing and full of joy, you are meant to be happy.

Of course, with all life's flotsam and jetsam there will be challenges, and you are meant to have them, because they help you to grow and by overcoming problems and challenges you will feel good about yourself.

Great challenges make life interesting; overcoming them makes life meaningful. Have fun with the challenges you face, joke about your troubles, laugh at your mistakes, learn from them, and gather strength from them.

Each wave will wash away an old layer of you and deposit treasures you never expected to find. Out goes inexperience, in comes awareness; out goes frustration, in comes resilience; out goes hatred, in comes kindness. No one would say these waves of emotional experience are easy to ride, but the rhythm of discomfort that you learn to tolerate is natural, helpful, and necessary. It leaves you stronger, healthier, and happier than it found you.

Keep practicing 'flipping' and it will improve the quality of your life immeasurably, you deserve and are meant to have an amazing life."

"Mahalo" thank you said Moana, "no worries, seestah" said Keli.

Many people are generous with others and really mean-spirited to themselves. They never give themselves any love; kindness, credit, care, grace, anything, or anytime for resting, recuperation, joy, spiritual renewal, learning, fun, balance, being alone, health or exercise.

Give yourself permission to do something you love to do; exercise, stop and have a quiet moment; go somewhere special to celebrate; play sport; have a bath; read a book; go surfing; hang out with friends; give yourself the gift of time.
-Amanda Gore

Wipeout:

"Splash and I swam out to the end of the lagoon, I sat on the wooden board, that I had found on the beach; I think it belonged to one of the older boys, I often watch them surf in the breakers beyond the reef, but father said I was still too young to go out there. But today I have Splash with me, and she believed that I will be okay." Said Moana.

The thunderous sound of the powerful waves crashing onto the reef made everything else hard to hear, how do we find a gap in the reef thought Moana, then she remembered a voice inside her head saying follow the turtles for they are a form of 'aumakua (spirit guardians), she looked around but could not see any turtles.

"Waves come in sets" said Splash, wait for a gap then paddle out "let's go" we paddled out over the flat rocks, and I could feel them with my hand as we glided smoothly over the top. Wow this is the first time I've been outside the lagoon; the water is really dark and blue out here thought Moana. She looked at Splash and smiled as she always did when Splash was around. Being a young dolphin, Splash knew how to have fun and Moana was one of her best friends, she had met Splash while playing in the lagoon, being small it was an area that Splash could access and escape the ever-watchful eyes of her parents.

"Let the first one go and catch the next wave" said Splash, with perfect timing Moana paddled hard, popped up onto her board and was riding the wave, "this is the best" she shouted "yippee" she was so happy, just then the wave broke and dumped its weight onto the hidden rocks below. Moana was pushed deep under water, she took a small knock, and found herself somewhere between two rocks, she almost had a little panic, she knew that the next wave might smash her against the bigger rocks, she had to get out, but how.

Then she heard Splash "don't panic" she said "compose yourself, clear your head, now focus and plan your move" which way is up? Thought Moana, when is the next wave? Do I have enough air? All of this flashed through her mind in a split second, and was instantly read by Splash, who replied telegraphically with, you're okay, bubbles up, you have plenty of air, stay under that rock and hold on tight to the seaweed, let the next wave pass then hold onto my fin and we will go up to the surface. With a plan in place Moana felt safe, she held onto the seaweed for dear life, the crashing wave was so powerful that she almost let go. As soon as it passed she swam out from under the rock placed her tiny hand onto the fin being offered by Splash, then only using her mind, she said, "go Splash go" and they took off for the surface.

Moana smiled widely as she passed through a spectrum of colour from deep blue to turquoise, the light sparkled on the surface above as they exploded out of the water like a shooting star, Splash span in the air, did a back flip and landed Moana right next to her surfboard. They were giggling loudly as they glided over the flat rock, back into the safety of the lagoon.

What Splash showed me today was very important, thought Moana. No matter how deeply in trouble I might find myself in, or how impossible the situation may first appear, the best thing to do is to take a deep breath (unless you are under water) clear your head, focus on looking for the best way forward and then commit, just go for it.

Mojo loved this story for it reminded him of a time back home when he had an argument with his mom. Angry and confused Mojo had confided in the local Kuma (teacher). The Kuma gave him some advice that he has used several times since and it had always worked, now Moana's story had validated his own.

The Kuma had said remember CAA (Calm Composure, Adapt, Action) anytime you find yourself in trouble, have a problem, or find yourself in uncomfortable situations apply the following:

Compose~ means to re-balance (Pono) to get real, and this is achieved by calming down and creating space. When waves of emotion bombard you as with an argument you can create space, either in your head by taking several deep breaths, or physically by walking away and finding somewhere quiet.

Adapt~ means assessing the situation, first ask yourself where am I in this situation and where do I want to be. Secondly come up with a plan, a route from where you are to where you want to be. Mojo was angry with his mom, but he didn't want to be angry with her, so the plan was to go back, say sorry and give her a hug.

Action~ means to take action, implement the plan. "Plan your work and work your plan" the Kuma had said. Mojo had returned home said sorry and gave his mom a hug just as he had planned, she then told him that she loved him very much and in turn gave him a big hug, balanced (pono) was restored to their relationship.

Just then it occurred to Mojo that this 'CAA' could also be used on his body, because he remembered visiting the therapist after twisting his ankle, she applied ice to reduce the inflammation which created space in the joint, she also gave a treatment plan to follow, one which they both worked at over the next few weeks, we actioned the plan. I'm getting the hang off this, thought Mojo, he then thanked Echo with a big Mahalo for yet another Moana story.

Splash:

Moana sat on the golden sand and looked out to sea with a big smile on her face, she started thinking about her new friend, a unique gift from the ocean. There was something very special about Splash, happy-go-lucky, she radiated joy, fun, and laughter.

Her sanguine demeaner was palatable, and she created sunshine for others to step into. She had a soft beauty and a twinkle in her big bright eyes. She looked familiar, and reminded Moana of someone, although she never knew who.

She was never afraid to show her appreciation outright, at others, at something in her day, at herself. Her attention went wave to wave, fish to fish, person to person, fully focused she surfed with grace on every wave, a vision floating on warm currents. She seemed at once childlike and yet more mature than anyone Moana know. She was very easy to please, because she took joy in the smallest things, but exacting too, because that small thing must be authentic, and wondrous in its small self. She was very complicated and at the same time, very simple.

She wants to see people happy and explained that a happy person expresses the greatest gratitude, just by being alive, in the moment, fully emersed in the now. Life is meant to be enjoyed; and it was in everybody's best interest to realize that their inner spirit is the source of all enjoyment.

That eternal spark of light residing inside your body has more energy than you will ever need, let your light shine bright into the world, be the best version of you, were ideas expressed by Splash.

Moana remembered advice that Splash once gave when she had been upset about something trivial. Don't worry about the past or the future for all your anxieties live there, live now, and enjoy, for in the present there are no worries or anxieties. The present can always be filled with joy, with love, and with aloha. If you were to fully live in the moment, for only a moment, the stress and strain of your entire life will be washed away, so go, and play in the surf.

Splash would often say "share the joy, have fun, be happy and be kind. It's important to help others and you help others most by being happy, it's very simple, the purpose of life is the expression of happiness."

I might try that unassuming way of sharing aloha, thought Mojo. From tomorrow I'm going to share the joy and try to leave a smile on someone's face each day and hopefully change the way they feel, for the better. Wow! Just the thought makes me feel excited, happy, and full of enthusiasm, sharing joy is sharing aloha, it's simple but not easy.

Starfish:

Moana was eager to get to the beach because there had been a storm last night, and all sorts of wonderful new playthings get wash ashore after a storm. She only had a few minutes before school started, in a flash she was gone, running through the lush green vegetation and around coconut trees, she then exploded onto the beach shouting "Ta Da!" to anyone who could hear her.

To her astonishment there was just one old man walking along the beach but thousands and thousands of starfish that had been washed ashore.

The old man was walking slowly and stooping often, picking up one starfish after another and tossing each one gently into the ocean. Moana ran up to the old man and asked, "Why are you throwing starfish into the ocean?".

"Because the sun is up, and the tide is going out and if I don't throw them further into the water they will die."

"But, old man, don't you realise this is a very long beach and there are starfish all along it! You can't possibly save them all, you can't even save one-tenth of them. In fact, even if you work all day, your efforts won't make a difference at all."

The old man listened calmly to Moana and then bent down to pick up another starfish, then he threw it into the sea.

"It has made a difference to that one" he said, realising that their efforts no matter how small can change lives by helping one starfish at a time, Moana ran back to the school told the Kuma (teacher) what she had seen.

Shouting with joy all the keiki (children) from the school ran down to the beach and spent the entire day with the old man, working together, singing happily and feeling good as they danced along the beach throwing starfish back into the ocean, step by step, starfish by starfish they learnt that you don't need to make a big gesture to make a big difference, just one small step and one small action can change the life of one starfish, and with many people taking just one small step, many lives can be change.

You know what thought Mojo I'm going to tell this story the next time we are asked to join in and help at a beach clean. If all the kids in our school pick up just one piece of plastic from our local beach, then like the starfish we can make a difference to the environment, plus we will have a clean beach.

(Adapted from Loren Eiseley)

Mino:

Gently swaying in his hammock and looking up above at the celestial canvas of the night sky Mojo couldn't help but smile, he felt good and was the happiest he had been since setting foot on the island.

Why? One word..... Mino

That's right, it's all because of Mino, (Minoaka) the cheeky little monkey that he met today. They had a fun time swinging in the trees, running through the long grass, Mino loved to play with Billy, and all three were laughing their heads off, as they enjoyed each other's company.

Mojo thought that the name Mino was ideal because it is short for Minoaka, which is Hawaiian for smiler and boy did he smile; his enthusiasm was infectious, he just makes everyone around him feel great, Mino's joy in finding new playmates had become overwhelming, and eventually he fall asleep tired but happy, he curled up and rested his head on Billy's tummy, he was feeling contented and safe being snuggled up against his new friend.

Mojo watched the stars dancing in the sky and thought to himself, that is what Mino does, he is so cheerful, so full of joy, that he radiates happiness, he lights up our lives, he just sparkles, and he makes us all feel alive. Mojo remembered that he once read that 'a smile is the passport, that kindness uses, to travel to your eyes, your heart, and your soul.'

Mojo thought 'how true, when I first met Mino earlier in the day, I was a bit down, I was feeling sorry for myself, nothing was going right, the stress of being on my own, just trying to survive was getting me down. But then I met Mino, and his smile is so infectious, I couldn't help but smile back and it change my mood, I started to feel better, then feel good, then feel happy, we had fun, we played and laughed all day. Somehow, I always feel better when thinking of others instead of just myself.

I must remember when I am feeling a little down, happiness is appreciating what you already have.'

With a big smile on his face Mojo sang a little ditty:

"From me to we, I'm telling you,

Will turn dark to light, when feeling blue.

With a smile on my face and feeling the light,

I'm happy now and bid you goodnight."

Pebble:

The wahine (women) of the village were preparing food for the evening meal when Moana got out of little-school, that day the lesson had been about learning to cook and she wanted to join in, to be a grown up and make a meal for the village.

Moana gathered a few sticks, some dry crispy leaves and made a small fire, something Gramma Tala had taught her to do using sea glass and sunrays. She then grabbed a small cooking pot, filled it with water and put it onto the fire, "what are you going to cook?" said the wahine as they watch her prepare. Moana placed her hand on a small white pebble inside her skirt pocket and instantly tuned into a memory collected long ago, one held within its structure, she placed the ancient pebble into the water "pebble soup" she shouted excitingly, "this is going to be the best soup ever and when it's done I'm going to share it with all of you" said Moana.

"That looks like a really good soup, can I add an onion?" said one of the women. "Yes please" said Moana.

"I'll be happy to get you one, and perhaps I can add a carrot as well?"

"That would be very nice" and the onions and carrots were added to the pot.

Soon, a small crowd started to assemble. "What are you making?", one of the onlookers asked.

"Why, soup, and it's made with only one small pebble! It will be delicious."

One of her classmates grumbled. "How can soup be delicious when made with only a pebble? that's crazy! It needs some beans and poi to make it rich. Here, let me get you some." He went away and returned shortly with beans and poi which he placed into the cooking pot. Seeing this, other villagers came with their gifts of meat, tomatoes, and other vegetables. The pot literally overflowed with contributions from the people.

As the pot filled and the wonderful smell drifted through the village, the crowd grew larger and larger, and everyone arriving was holding a small bowl, eventually Moana shouted, "the soup is ready." Everyone was served with a bowl of the delicious soup, and as the pot emptied Moana pulled out her small white pebble and one person in the crowd exclaimed: "Mahalo (Thank you), Moana for your soup. It was the best we have ever had. And to think, it was made with only one pebble!"

When re-telling the story Moana's Kuma (teacher) said "wonderful things can be made from small beginnings, if we all contribute a little something."

Squishy:

"What are you doing, I'm looking for Squishy, what's a Squishy? It's a sea sponge with a face on it! Are you mad?" said Mojo to himself as he walked along the seashore, well it would not be the first time something weird has happened on this island, said the voice in his head, as he thought about the Moana story that he had heard earlier in the day.

"Hello Echo" said Moana, "Look what I found it's a big yellow sea sponge and the flower markings on it looks like a face, it's all soft and squishy, that's it I'm going to call it Squishy; it can be my new pillow and I'm going to cuddle it when I go to sleep" Moana now had a new friend, one born in her imagination, but needing her to bring it alive.

Moana pretended to go to sleep resting her head on her Squishy, and before she knew it she had indeed fallen asleep. As she entered the land of nod Squishes' eyes opened, her long lashes tickled Moana and she let out a little giggle, then Squishy whispered into the small pearl shaped ear resting upon her, "I'm your new friend, hug me, cuddle me, squish me, whenever you need me and I will wrap you in a soft comfy cloud, one that feels warm, cosy, and safe".

"Let me tell you something Moana" said azura, the spirit found in the cave had joined the conversation.

'The ocean holds the great power of transformation, it has the ability to absorb negative energy and reground us, it is a great healer. When things get a little crazy simply make a splash, jump into the ocean and all your landlocked problems will disappear. It's just you and the sea, your body will soften as you become yielding and flexible like water itself. Anxieties are washed away, and every cell is tuned to the sea. It's a process of forgetting while also remembering what's truly important. The heartbeat steadies and breathing relaxes as you feel the ocean flowing through your soul, you no longer feel like a drop in the ocean, but the entire ocean in a drop, a sense of oneness.

The feeling of calm that encapsulates a chaotic mind when squeezing, cuddling, or hugging a Squishy is a true portrayal of the power of aloha, it creates a wave of feel good energy that surrounds you, an electromagnetic wave of positive energy, you will feel calm, contented, happy, you will radiate happy waves, you will give off good vibes, and in return good vibes will be attracted to you, just like a magnet.

Walk barefoot across the hot sand, put your toes in the saltwater, bathe with Squishy and let the feeling of connection with nature revitalise you.'

Following a story like that Mojo thought back to when he was little and how much he loved his 'Otto Minion' it gave him the same kind of comfort, now he just had to find his own Squishy, the midday sunlight danced upon the glassy water as he waded through the swallows, fish, shells, coral, all the trappings of an aqua paradise but no squishy sponge in sight, step by watery step followed by gentle ripples he slowly made his way along the length of the bay, footprint after footprint being washed away by the oceans kiss.

"You can cuddle, snuggle, hug and squeeze, but an extra squish makes everything special, you are my squishy" said Mojo to Billy as he repeated Moana's words.

"Friendships are incredibly important for mental health, providing social support, connection and community."
-Dr Jay Watts, a Clinical Psychologist, Psychotherapist

Lia Tree:

"Today marks a change of season" said the Kuma (teacher) "and in one months' time the village will have a celebration, our part in that event is to design a picture of a Plumeria tree in the sand." She went on to explain that the Frangipani flowers of the Plumeria tree are used to make Lia's (flower necklace) and when the flowers have all dropped the tree branches will look like fingers of coral. Therefore, the job of the Keiki (children) is to collect sticks of driftwood and broken branches and create a full-size model of a plumeria tree lying flat on the sand. "Then when the leaf's and petals drop, you have to collect everyone and place them on the model of the tree, don't forget to put a small pebble on each leaf to prevent it from blowing away" said the Kuma.

How are we going to collect all the leaf's there are just too many of them, we can't possibly collect all of them, the task is too big, can't we not just make just one Lia, protested the Keiki. The prospect of the project weighted heavily on their minds, they slumped in their chairs and looked unhappy, the limitation of their minds created stress within their bodies.

"Okay" said the Kuma, "listen up; Failure is a feeling long before it becomes an actual result, you can do this. There are three thousand leaves and petals that need collecting, we have ten Keiki in the school, which means each one of you will collect three hundred leaves and petals over the next thirty days, that is only ten leaves a day for each one of you to pick up, can you do that?" said the teacher.

"Yes!" they all shouted with excitement "we can do that."

Moana stood up and said, "if we all collect ten flowers each, on our way to school in the morning, we will have collected one hundred between us and we can then start making our Lia, then the next day if we do the same, we can join the Lia's making a chain, let's all make that promise" all the Keiki gathered into a circle put their hands together and said, "we promise to work together, collect flowers and leaf's every day and not break the chain." They were happy again, with a smile on their face and a song in their heart, they ran and skipped into the long grass to play.

Gramma Tala looked at the Kuma and said, "that was very cleaver, you shifted their focus away from what seemed like a large unachievable goal and placed it onto a fun and doable daily ritual, one that would eventually achieve the goal" "yep! You can get anywhere and achieve anything, by just taking one small step in the right direction every day, the secret is to reduce the step to an achievable size, then take that first step, followed by repeat and repeat, just keep going, day after day" said the Kuma.

They both smiled at each other and laughed as they went their separate ways.

Mojo loved this story he had been putting off building the canoe because the job just seemed too big, a too hard a task. Now he thought I'm going to start building it tomorrow, I'm going to find or cut one log, just one log, then I'm going to do the same every day, until I have enough for my craft, and I'll make rope and a sail from weaving coconut palms together. Maybe I'll have it done before someone finds me, then I can leave this island and go home.

Go Splash a little joy, have fun, be kind. Share aloha, give love to others through kindness, encouragement, support, gratitude, and to do it with no thought of any reward is living the aloha way. The magic is it comes back to you and multiplies itself, bringing aloha to every other area of your life. -azura

Hoppi:

Moana was crying as she spoke into the ear of Echo. "Last week Hoppi died, I loved him sooo much, he has been by my side my whole life and now he has gone, it's not fair. I've been crying for a whole week, I just can't stop, and it still hurts." She had struggled to overcome the waves of sadness that just kept pushing her under, taking her down into a dark place.

My Gramma Tala said, "Grief is the price we pay for love. So, grieve and mourn for a while wash the pain out of your system. Then as soon as you can, focus on how grateful you are to have known him, feel appreciation for what he gave you, and then send him love and gratitude.

Hoppi knows you miss him, and he loves you, he does not want to see you suffering and in pain, that just makes him unhappy. Think of the good times you had, all the fun and laughter, the love you shared for each other and be grateful for that experience, it will make you feel better, and it will make Hoppi feel better, he lives inside your heart and his spirit will share your joy and smiles in the years ahead. Remember when you find it hard to be happy focus on the joy that he brought into your life and be grateful for that one thing.

Sometimes we all feel like there is nothing to be grateful for, but it's not really true. If you can walk, talk, see, or breathe, that's a good place to start.

You have a gift of 86,400 seconds each day, have you used anyone of them to say Mahalo, thank you to Hoppi for being in your life. Be thankful for all the little things, this will lead to a trickle of gratitude and continuous gratitude will led to a splash of joy, do this and his memory will last longer than his life".

I still get waves of sadness, sometimes even waves of madness, when I just want to scream and shout. Sometimes there are no waves, just flatness and a pain in the stomach. I want to focus on the joy he gave, but I feel guilty if I'm not grieving, it's as if my pain is a measure of my love for him. I feel that if I'm not in pain then I was not in love, kinda mixed up I know.

I know that feeling guilty about feeling happy, it stops us feeling joy, and that joy is the unbridled expression of his spirit dancing to our shared heartbeat of love and life. I also know that the path from waves of pain, to waves of joy starts with a positive action, I know all this, but it's still hard.

"Living actively is actively grieving, honouring your loved one by living life to the full in a way that they would have wished for you" said, Gramma Tala.

It is said that the 'dash' between the date of your birth, and the date of your death, represents your life as we dash from day to day forever chasing, the things we think we need. Change your dash to a splash, slow down, take a cleansing breath and enjoy your life, appreciate all the little things, for they hold the seeds of happiness.

"Go Splash, have fun, be kind, and share the joy with your friends" said Gramma Tala. It's her way of saying go surf, play, laugh, share aloha, socialise, and help others, this is the first step to healing.

From aloha comes gratitude, from gratitude comes compassion, from compassion comes kindness, from kindness comes love, from love comes aloha. A complete circle of life, to have loved and to have been loved, this is the aloha way.

"Today I have decided to be sad, grief for a while; then I'm going to live and live well, for the spirit of Hoppi lives inside of me and he shares my life with me, good and bad, happy, or sad. Together we are going to make happy memories."

Gramma Tala once said, "don't take life for granted, and don't take the people in your life for granted" Moana then made a vow.

"I'm going to be kind to myself, ride happy waves, share joyful enthusiasm, touch the lives of those around me and make them feel better. Then I'm going to smile and make Hoppi's memories, magic ones, this is the gift of grief" whispered Moana into her secret shell "Mahalo."

Then as always she took her problem to the sea in the hope that the waves will wash them away.

"The aim of surf therapy is not to teach people to be surfers. It's to get them to use surfing to change their brain chemistry." -Darryl Virotko

Happy Days:

Days have turned into weeks, and weeks have turned into months, time slipped by slowly, and days drifted without names, why has someone not found me yet? I don't know how long I am going to be here, but I am having fun, thought Mojo. Soon it will be the end of the summer break and I will be expected back at school, then someone will come looking.

Like anyone stuck on an island Mojo had developed a daily routine, he spent his time fishing, cooking, sleeping, and playing with Billy and Mino, and at low water he would have fun with is aqua friends. He had made a camp at the edge of the beach using driftwood and palm leaves, from there he could see the lagoon and beyond out into the bay. At the far end of the beach, on a high rock he had carefully constructed fire ready to be lit at a moment's notice, next to this signal fire sat a huge pile of leaves, some dry ready for burning and some green for smoke, he was hoping to find a conch shell, one that didn't speak, to use as a horn, but that search still continues.

Behind the high rock a large section of the reef was exposed at low tide creating a little spit of land separating the ocean from the beach, and revelling a field of coral and purple urchins, making it almost impossible to walk on without foot protection, Mojo had made himself a pair of reef shoes from palm leaves and vines which gave him license to explore this mysterious land of miniature waterfalls, streams of receding sea water sucking up and spilling over itself, thin sheaths of aqua blue creating little vortices and enhancing the vibrant colours of the living reef glistening in the sunlight.

But the part of the day Mojo looks forward to the most is when he can access the cave and listen to Moana's stories, carefully preserved within the vibration chambers of Echo's inner ear. Water dripped from the rocks and time stood still as Moana shared stories about her time growing up on the island and the long sunny days spent on the beach with her 'surf and sand' school friends, made this the happiest of childhoods, and Mojo could always feel, and almost touch, the energy of her spirit and the aloha she was sharing with her sweet words. She knew that if you want more joy and purpose in your life, then you have to take positive action and she was going to grow up to be a true leader of her people, the advice, and lessons she gained while playing on that beach would help her achieve her purpose and touch her destiny.

Yesterday's story was still ringing in Mojos ears, he kept playing it over and over again inside is head, as though the meaning might disappear if not continuously repeated. When she was a teenager Moana worried about her purpose in life and whether she was good enough to for fill her destiny. Gramma Tala had told Moana don't chase riches, adulation, power, or fame, for all these things will distract you from your life's purpose.

Be true to yourself, follow your heart, stay balanced and ride your own wave, for at the end there are only two things you take with you when your life is done, there are only two things that matter.

Moana said "Gramma please tell me what are the two things that really matter in life, what are they."

Gramma Tala lent towards Moana and whispered in her ear "To love, and to have been loved.

For to love, and to have been loved, reflects a life full of aloha and that's all there is. We live in this ocean of emotion, we will encounter giant waves of anger, frustration, jealousy, resentment and even hatred, all will test us, but our job is to survive the storm and find the love in a new dawn.

You are spirit embodied in human form, you are here for no other reason other than to surf the wave of love, and to grow from the experience. That's all there is and all you will take with you.

Ask yourself am I loved, and do I love, with all my heart?" Job complete!

"The best surfer out there is the one having the most fun."
-Duke Kahanamoku

Waters of Life:

Sitting on a large rock contemplating, Mojo had many thoughts running through his head, most of them just increased his stress levels. How am I going to get off this island? Will someone find me? Has anyone missed me yet? When will my boat be finished? What are the Banga boys going to do when they catch me?

"He wai e ola" said a voice,

"what" exclaimed Mojo,

"The waters of life" repeated the voice.

Mojo looked at the group of rocks next to him and saw one move, then an old leathery head appeared from within, and smiled.

Wow! This place, thought Mojo, now the turtles are even talking to me, what next?

"Hi, I'm Connie you must be Mojo" said the turtle "and I hear your thoughts, the waters of life is a phrase we use to help you understand that life is not static, its dynamic, fluid, like the ocean, life is constantly changing. It's a huge, overpowering, and awesome force. You cannot hope to live for any extended time in the ocean. You can surf there, swim out there, and survive for a brief period of time, but unless you've got a canoe, a good solid boat underneath you, you cannot survive indefinitely in the ocean. It's just too big."

"Exactly!" said Mojo, "Where do I start, what am I supposed to do?"

"Life's circumstances are like the waves, constantly in motion. They go up and down, in and out; they're calm or they're rough. They are what they are. When you are in your canoe, you're riding the waves, feeling safe in your own space, no matter what the sea is doing around you, you are in Pono (balance). Pono is about obtaining balance in life, doing the right thing, it's about being in harmony with the environment, internally and externally. It doesn't describe life's situations; it describes your reactions to them" said Connie.

It's very clear cut, black and white, you are either in the canoe or in the water, you're either in Pono or you're not, you're either balancing on your surfboard riding the waves or you're in the sea trying to get back onto the board. Sometimes you might just be trying to survive the pounding of the waves and need help getting back onboard, never be afraid to ask for help.

We always know when we are in Pono. We know when we're reacting to life in a calm, connected manner, and we know when we are not.

No one has to tell us when we fall out of the canoe or off our board. We're all wigged out, mind racing, heart pounding, gut clenched, in survival mode. Shit happens! Pono is about regaining balance, getting back onboard, learning to overcome reactionary, unconscious behaviours, no matter how high or hard the seas of life are tossing you, and it all starts with aloha.

Do the right thing. If something doesn't feel right in your gut, it's not right. Your mind can produce ten different reasons why it is, but deep down in your gut, when something doesn't feel right, it isn't.

The waves on the ocean are often turbulent for those without an anchor. Until you find your anchor, you'll always be prone to seasickness, Pono can be an anchor for you, but remember this you can't drop an anchor in a wave, look for the valleys between the waves for they hold an opportunity to quieten the mind, change the emotion and refresh the soul.

Mojo looked at Connie, smiled and said "Mahalo." He was from an island culture whose world was essentially tiny bits of land surrounded by a vast expanse of ocean and using 'the waters of life' as a metaphor for understanding the waves of thoughts and feelings that we are constantly dealing with, as we try to stay afloat on this ocean of emotion, can be a great way of obtaining balance and staying in Pono. And one that Mojo understood, perfectly, but the valleys where do we find the valleys? "In the breath" said Connie, "when emotions take over, stop! Breathe, slowly and deeply, one for the mind, one for the body and one for the soul, this will give you composure."

"Being in the moment, everything becomes more intensive, energy fills your body, it's the best feeling in the world. Somethings are scared and cannot be described, that's why I think surfing is a spiritual thing. For me life is love, and love is the glue, which holds the universe together, and love manifests itself in art of surfing.

Follow your heart, follow your feelings, have a romance with the ocean, slowly and in time you will learn to read her moods. The main problem in the world is a lack of love, and riding waves of aloha is an act of love."

"The waters of life" said Mojo aloud, "I get it, I really do!"

Sometimes in the waves of change, we find our direction.
-azura

Finding Focus:

'I sat on a large surfboard, the bigger the board the easier it is to surf. The day was warm, and the tide was out, and I was able to wade to the line-up. Not three seconds after I got there, a wave appeared on the horizon. Muscle memory took over. I spun my board around, paddled twice, and popped up to my feet. I dropped into that wave, then dropped into another dimension, one that I did not know even existed.

The first thing I noticed was that time had slowed to a crawl. My brain was working at normal speed, but the world was going by in freeze frame. My vision was panoramic. It felt like I could see the back of my head. Then I realised I didn't seem to have a head. Or not exactly. There was a body travelling on a surfboard across a wave, but the rider was missing. My sense of self had vanished. My consciousness had expanded outward. I had merged with the ocean, become one with the universe.' -Scott Stillman.

This is me, thought Mojo as he sat on his makeshift board following a fun hour in the surf, the sun now drying the water on his skin, to salt.

This is definitely me, he exclaimed, as he remembered the feelings expressed by a surfer in a mag he had recently read.

Waves of fear and depression had descended earlier in the day. Worried about his future, his ability to survive, will he ever be found? Mojo was drowning in big waves of emotion, each heavy wave came crashing down with the full force hopelessness, he was slowly sinking into the dark depths of depression. Mojo began to feel sorry for himself, what have I done to deserve this? It's not fair? Why me? With each dark thought came a fresh wave of dread.

Then he remembered the mantra he had been told "Go Splash, be joyful, have fun, be kind." But I don't want to, I don't want to do anything thought Mojo.

"You get what you focus on" said a voice inside his head, "focus can be either friend or foe, focus on scarry things and you will find yourself swimming in waves of fear, focus on the joy in your life and happy waves will appear, it all comes down to focus and mindset."

'Rather than fearing what I don't want, I'm focusing on what I do want. Like a surfer training to catch the perfect break, I'm building skills, sense, and sensitivity to ride this wave of change.' -Roz Savage

Mojo closed his eyes and took a deep breath, as a previous lesson came back to him. Stay calm, compose yourself and create a gap, a gap between feeling depressed and a desire to feel better, breathe the soothing blue light of the azura into the space, and feel the calming wave of aloha gently flowing through your body.

Everything in the universe is composed of energy vibrating in various pattens, and your thoughts are forms of that energy. The one thing over which you have control is where you place your conscious attention, and focus is a powerful force – may the force be with you!

"May you live all the days of your life" -Jonathon Swift.

Energy flows where attention goes, both positive attitudes and positive expectation generate positive emotion. The thoughts you think and the feelings that follow them have an electromagnetic reality, the concentration of your attention sets up a vibration of energy, and we have to learn to ride waves of this positive energy to nurture and support its flow.

Focus on the moment, this moment and only this moment, to do that, go splash, play, laugh, and smile with all your heart, then you will create a moment of magic and experience a flow of aloha. At first this might be a small micro-flow, one that changes moods, emotions, and feelings for the better. If you can repeat this trick and build magic moments upon magic moments you may even get a full-blown state of macro-flow, a quasi-mystical experience where not only does the impossible become possible, but it becomes just another thing you do.

So, when in dread, to get out of your head... you need to get up out of your bed, go, and enjoy the flow.

"Being in nature quiets my mind, and out of that quietness is where the real art happens" -David Eisenhour (Sculptor)

Fun of Focus:

Living on this tropical island garden, the children of the rainbow seemed to communicate with a sense way beyond the basic human senses, one that allowed them to connect to nature and the world around them as easily as they connect person-to-person.

"This is fun" said Moana as she sat on the beach with Pua and a couple of friends from school. They had invented a new game which they called 'find my shell' and this is how it works, lying on the sand was a pile of seashells with distinctive individual markings, Moana would pick one while everyone else had their eyes closed, she then had one minute to describe the shell, this required observation, concentration, and focus.

"This beautiful shell is small and white, it has ribs fanning out from a single point, each rib has a aqua glow, and at the bottom right corner a grey smudge can be seen, the inside is pearl white and shiny in kinda soft way" Said Moana, "now open your eyes and see who is the first to find the shell." Giggling the keiki quickly sifted through the pile of shells until one shouted "found it" then it was her turn.

They would play this game for hours, especially on days when the sea was rough and access to the lagoon was not possible.

Moana had often watched the elders participate in a very special activity called Kamalamalama (light of knowledge) where they try to develop an ability to use the power of the total mind, this remarkable skill is achieved by engaging in the practice of expanded sensory perception using similar techniques she would later design her 'find my shell' game on.

We all live by using five basic senses: sight, smell, taste, touch, and hearing. Primarily these are used to survive and find our way in the world. A sixth sense, a 'psychic' sense that can be developed by expanding one or more of our basic senses. The elders on the island had developed the ability to concentrate completely on the present moment, focusing their mind on one subject, one object, or one thought, and at the same time exclude from the mind every other unrelated thought, idea, feeling, and sensation.

One of the elders was a fisherman and after watching him make fishhooks, Moana asked, "how do you manage to keep your attention on the task at hand and not let your mind wonder, I'm always thinking of other things." He said, "When I make my fishhooks, I think only about my fishhooks. I think about how smooth they are becoming, how the angles are coming out, how sharp the edge is, and what colour they are taking on. I don't think about how I will use them or how many fish I will catch. When I'm a hook maker, I'm a hook maker. When I'm a fisherman, I fish."

After hearing this story, Mojo thought how different it was on his island, he would go skateboarding while listening to music on his headphones, all the time trying to miss people on the sidewalk distracted by their cell phones. His house was mad at mealtimes, everyone was talking all at once, the TV would be on, and the iPad was also being used at the same time as the food was being consumed, it was always chaos, and very stressful.

It occurred to him that instead of expanded sensory perception they were all engaged in a diminishing sensory practice, one where their minds were busy, busy, busy, doing nothing. He thought that folks on his home island don't observe and respect their surroundings, and don't seem to have the time or ability to slow down and enjoy the fun of focusing on one thing at a time.

His mind then switched to auntie and how contented she was, she always appeared to have fun just focusing on her animals and vegetables, he remembered her saying "once you discover the thing you love doing, (your passion) pursuing it, and nurturing it every day will bring meaning to your life. The moment your life has this purpose you will achieve a happy state of being. Don't waste time regretting the past or worrying about the future, just focus on what you are doing right now, do the best you can and make today worth remembering."

She's right thought Mojo, athletes participating in sports will focus deeply when engaged in competition, artist will merge into their creations, children will have no concept of time while playing, and people who focus on the beauty of nature and spend their time bathing in its embracing energy, have all experienced their fishhook moment.

I love that, thought Mojo, as he collected seaweed, shells, twigs, pebbles and about anything that he could use to make his own game of focus.

"Surfing and life can be defined as how well you can stay in balance" -Sam Bleakley

Moments:

The ebb and flow of life helps us to connect with the oceans elements, wind, water, and waves, life is like the ocean thought Mojo.

Some days the water is calm, with tiny ripples flowing seamlessly to the shore, and other times the waves are big, crashing and pounding. Sometimes like today the waves are just so big and wild, you're better off standing on the shore and observing. Today was windy and the once blue sky was full of clouds. Mojo stared at natures ever changing canvas, and he tried to make an island come out of the slow-moving sea of clouds.

At first it looked like a small shell afloat on the water. Then it grew larger and was a beautiful swan with unfolding wings. Then in the rising sun it became a ship. Mojo jumped up full of excitement, he shouted as loud as he could, but the wind drowned his voice, the waves were high and beating against the rocks with the sound of thunder, the fire, I must light the fire thought Mojo as he jumped down from the rocks and rushed along the shore to the readily prepared signal fire. He grabbed the fire stick which had carefully been wrapped in dry palm leaves and poked it into the embers of last night's bonfire, it burst into flames, with his heart pumping aloud Mojo took one last look at the ship.

Startled, he looked again towards the now wobbly horizon, the ship had become a soft white cloud sitting on the sea, the fluffy cloud gently transformed into cherry blossom adrift on the breeze and floated up into the heavens, the ocean once again became a desert of waves, a wilderness of water with a thousand-hues blending seamlessly from sea to sky.

Mojo felt the sand under his feet and dropped to his knees, waves of emotion tumbled in one after another in no special order, unpredictable as the ocean, his hands were submerged in the sea, as though trying to draw the stillness of the water through himself.

Breathe in 2,3,4. Hold 2,3,4. Breathe out 2,3,4. Relax 2,3,4. Mojo remembered aunties breathing technique for navigating life's ups and downs, then he again heard her voice.

"Stress can drain your energy fast. Imagine a boat drifting on the ocean, the current takes you to the past or future. A mindful moment is like throwing down an anchor, the boat becomes still not drifting between past and future but still in the present. There you will feel grounded, centred, and connected to all those around you, focus your attention and awareness on what's happening right now, moment to moment, breathe in 2,3,4 become more present in the now. This technique helps us to accept the present moment of reality without judgement, which nurtures greater awareness, clarity, and self-acceptance.

Relax like a seal laying on its back in the warm lagoon, floating up and down to the motion of the waves. Hold 2,3,4. Breathe out 2,3,4. Relax 2,3,4".

Mojo became relaxed, very relaxed, his mind drifted, then words slid gently into his head.

The spectacular vitality of the sea ignites my own. Senses come alive, the whooshing crash of waves, the salt-crusted air, the rocking of my body, rising and falling with rolling swells. Great peace descends as her waves lull me back to life, recalibrating my internal rhythms. I become formless, shapeless like the sea. All the while, I'm exercising balance, honing intuition, cultivating awareness. -Scott Stillman

That's how I feel though Mojo, he then opened his eyes, his tears replaced by saltwater, he smiled and said, "Mahalo auntie, I love you."

Make time to be fully present with the most important people in your life, even if you only have five minutes, it's still a wonderful gift. Make them feel special, hear them with your heart and they will feel loved. -Amanda Gore

Waves of Aloha:

On a warm sunny afternoon Mojo found himself drifting on a log in the calm tranquil water of the lagoon, the fragrance of the salty air and the gentle soothing motion of the waves were slowly rocking him to sleep.

When the mind is calm it's like warm water, relaxing every cell with its gentle ripples, you feel clam, contented and at one within your world.

Feeling peaceful, safe, and supported by his surroundings, his thoughts wandered back to what Moana had shared in her diary only hours before.

"Today I learned about waves of aloha" said a familiar voice. Our Kuma (teacher) told us that there are only two groups of emotional waves, negative ones, and positive ones. We as humans are wired to seeing and riding negative waves, it is part of our primal survival system, we notice and react to negative experiences more than positive ones.

Focusing on a vibration of negative waves may keep us alert and alive, but when the waves are too strong it will increase our stress to extreme levels. When this happens, we become more sensitive to the negative and find ourselves caught up in a strong current of negative waves, that could led to unhappiness and depression.

If we have more negative things than positive things in our life, then something is wrong.

When we wake up in the morning we are either emotion free (calm water) or feel happy (positive mood/wave) or stressed (negative mood/wave) with the thought of what might happen in the coming day. We can choose to ride the wave, good or bad, happy, or sad, or we can simply let it go and re-balance.

To create balance, we should seek out the energy waves contained in good vibrations.

To do this we need to stop focusing on the negative by replacing it with an intense, novel, powerful and positive action (like surfing, or sport). The body's reaction of achieving this will activate happiness waves in the brain, which then are strengthened by repeating the activity, again and again, making it more sensitive to seeking and finding more positive waves".

"I'm always happy, or I'm mostly happy, except for the times I'm not" said Moana. "It's because Gramma Tala and I play with waves of aloha every day." Aloha is an unseen flow of energy and as real as air and water. It is an acting, living, moving energy force, it moves in waves and currents like these in the ocean. Some people say that aloha is love, but it's much, much more than that, because aloha is not just a feeling, aloha is a positive life force, your soul expressing itself through physical form.

A single wave of aloha has the power to change your life for the better. Give aloha (love, gratitude, compassion, and kindness) through thoughts, feelings, words, and actions. Fill your day with joy, fun and laughter and you will receive back a life full of positive things, for joy is the voice of aloha.

Every wave has an ebb and flow, one that goes out and comes back in. Give positivity and you will receive back positivity; give negativity and you will receive back negativity. It's your thoughts and feelings that determine whether your words and actions will be positive or negative, you literary choose the energy wave that you ride.

Choose waves of aloha.

Mojo was relaxed and kept his eyes closed and remembered a summers evening when auntie was sitting around a log fire and sharing her view about flowing with aloha. "Give the best of you. Your love, your joy, your positivity, your excitement, your gratitude, your passion, and you will flow with aloha" she said. Mojo nodded, smiled, and just felt great, in this moment life was good, his mind drifted as he floated in the warm embrace of the lagoon.

People say they want is happiness. But what they really want is joy, to be joyful, there is a vast difference between happiness and joy.

Happiness is often a reaction to an external event, whereas joy comes from the soul, it's your inner light, your spirit expressing itself via the body.

"I'm a firm believer that joy has everything to do with the health of your body. I feel like the body is an organism that is fed by the mind" – Sheryl Crow.

Happiness isn't out there, waiting to be found, it's in you, waiting to be embraced. Find Joy and you will ride your own wave of aloha, and if you embrace that wave you'll get the best ride of your life.

"Joy is the profound contentment and peace that comes when you are able to enjoy nature and her magnificence. It's the ability to love yourself and others, to be compassionate and generous, the enthusiasm for life that comes from focusing on gratitude. It's the sense of fulfilment when you have genuinely helped someone else, when you change the way that others feel, for the better." – Amanda Gore.

The Key: (The nerdy bit)

"Come take a seat and listen for we have little time" said azura, her gentle voice overflowing with aloha, vibrated around the cave, and filled Mojo with a supreme sense wellbeing.

"Soon you will be on your way home, and I have a gift for you, you wanted to know why you had voices in your head. Understanding the answer is without doubt the key to choosing happy waves and obtaining a happy life."

Already Mojo had several questions, why have we got little time, when will I be going home, how will I get home?

But before he could respond the show began, visions appeared in the cave, streaks of lightening flashed across the small space striking hard rock and sending veins of electricity around the walls. One strike created a patten of the demigod Maui, the image was singing and dancing as though he was on hot coals. Turning first into a bright light with an intense white core Maui shapeshifted into a hologram, a bee full of electricity, "I'm a buzz, a vibration of energy" said Maui "come join me" and in that instant he pointed at Mojo and sent a bolt of lightning straight into his chest, sparks flew, the cave lit up and a startled Mojo had also turned into a small bee, he was but a single spark of electricity. "Wa-hee, this is fun" exclaimed Maui while touching Mojo on the nose, a move that resulted in both of them shrinking to a dot, a pin head, then even smaller. "Follow me" said Maui, motioning

Mojo to follow as he entered the ear of a Polynesian warrior who had appeared in the cave.

They were inside his head, seeking out the nooks and crannies, wow I can see an image of myself sitting in the cave thought Mojo as he looked out from the warriors eyes. The warrior took in a deep breath, one that threw them both into the back of this head, with a bump their translucent bodies morphed into a higher vibration, a thought resting within the brain. Then a transcript, an explanation started.

Our internal environment is connected to, and influenced by, the external environment via our five senses (some say six or even seven). It is through this radar system that we gather information of events and happenings going on around us, this information then enters our nervous system.

Here two things happen simultaneously, first our bodyguard (fight, flight response) checks for danger (your brain is not designed to make you happy, its designed to keep you safe, and help you survive) and second the non-important and non-relevant information is deleted. This is because our brains can take in millions of bits of information, but we can only actually process a few per second.

Next this wave of information will go through our personal filters, these are constructed by our values, beliefs, education, culture, memories, and experience. Because no two people have the same life experience, no two sets of filters are the same. That's why two people can witness the same event yet experience it differently.

Information here is either, deleted, diluted, distorted, generalised, or stored based on our filters. What we end up with, is a very personalised version of reality, it can never be the actual event because we change reality as it goes through our filters. Our filters are memories from information received, consciously and unconsciously, they are self-limiting in nature.

Now, at this point, we have created a thought from information received via the senses, what happens next, is that we apply an emotion to the thought, which in turn triggers a chemical response. If it's a happy thought then the body will produce happy hormones (chemicals) so that you can experience feeling happy.

Your brain is like a pharmacy dispensing chemicals at all hours. Every thought you have produces a biochemical reaction. The chemicals can be either negative or positive depending on the emotion that you attach to the thought, they then circulate around the body via the bloodstream, as neurotransmitters, this is the mind-body connection at work.

Circulation of the chemicals create moods; we are now experiencing feelings of our thoughts. Our feelings good or bad generate more emotions positive or negative, in a continuous feedback loop, which can sometimes result in a high discharge of emotion such as, frustration, anger, love, and happiness.

Waves of emotions, thoughts, and feelings will constantly flow, they will take you high and take you low. They will lift you up and they will knock you down, they will not stop, that is guaranteed.

Your emotions generated by your thoughts are responsible for the chemicals that your body is releasing, whether they enhance your well-being or are harmful to body and mind.

If you are thinking depressing, fearful, guilty, or angry thoughts, you are actually harming yourself. Nobody else is doing it to you, it is self-inflicted.

Now the good news.

You can learn to control the controllable's.

You can't control what happens to you, but you can control how you choose to respond. You can learn to ride the waves of feelings and emotions.

If you only remember one thing, remember this:

You cannot feel happy and sad at the same time, you can be happy and sad, but you cannot feel it, that's because there is chemistry involved. The power found within this statement is immense, for it means you can choose your mood, at any moment, at any time, you can choose how you feel.

The trick is to focus on what you want, and not on what you don't want. How do you want to feel? If you want to feel happy then focus on a happy memory, event, person, or pet, remember the moment that made you smile, remember how it felt, remember how it made you feel inside, capture that feeling, breathe it in, you are now creating your own new wave of energy, the body will respond by producing the required chemicals, to match the mood you have chosen. Don't forget to put a smile on your face even if it's a false silly grin, it will still affect the way you feel. It is impossible to feel bad when having good happy thoughts.

Sometimes we choose to ride the waves of grief, sadness, and depression, and that's also okay. We are here to experience the full range of human emotions, just make sure it's the right emotion at the right time, balance is the key.

The mind is the thinking part of the brain it deals with the flow of information from sensory input to interpretation and the creation of emotions and feelings.

Your mind creates foods for moods.

At this moment Mojo remembered a quote from the reggae singer Bob Marley 'None but ourselves can free our mind, feeling pretty please with himself, he turned his attention back to the cinematic show evolving before his eyes.

'So much for chemicals, now let's look at voices in your head' this is more like it, thought Mojo.

Ancient Polynesian culture talks about man having three minds or three thinking aspects of the mind. In 2002 D--n-y brought out 'Lilo & Stitch' a film about a dysfunctional Hawaiian family consisting of young Lilo and her older sister Nani, they adopt a failed alien experiment impersonating as a dog who they named 'Stitch'. Now if we adapt this story it becomes a fun way of exploring and explaining the functions of all three aspects of the of the mind.

Listen carefully for in this story you will find the way too living a balanced and happy life, should you choose to surf a wave of aloha.

Lilo is a seven-year-old child and represents the part of the mind that we identify as us, the human thinking, caring, educated aspect, we will return to Lilo later. Nani is the older sister, and her job is to protect the family (our embodiment) which she does with the only tools available to her, Fight, Flight, or Freeze. Then we have Stitch a pet alien identifying as a dog, Stitch is strong, intelligent, fisty, temperamental, aggressive, and concerned with self-preservation, Stitch knows what he wants, and wants it, when he wants it.

Imagine that we have the three members of the family living in our head and all three have a voice. Let's now look at each one, see how they work, and try to figure out how we can help them to become harmonized and balanced. (pono)

Let's start with Stitch:

Stitch is the part of your mind that acts without permission. When you tell stories or lie, when you are mean, grumpy, naughty, or bossy. When you get annoyed, angry, or throw toddler tantrums, then you know that Stitch is misbehaving. Remember that Stitch is very strong and almost indestructible, if Stitch is left to play on its own, then crazy things start to happen. Stitch (much like a dog) will overreact when it feels that something is wrong, it will judge and act irrationally, and doesn't care if anyone or everyone, looks foolish.

Stitch has the ability to drown you in big oversize waves of negative emotion, such as rage, fear, victimization, worthlessness, jealously, guilt, sorrow, and depression. When caught in an emotional storm, Stitch will not respond to intelligent, or rational thoughts, and good intentions will mean less than nothing.

When Stitch is hurt, emotionally or physically he feels under attack, he gets angry, and goes into fighting mode, his reaction to stress is to hit out, shout, stamp, and vent his frustrations, often on the nearest person even if they are not responsible for his outburst. His actions are usually met with an equal reaction from those targeted, resulting in a shouting match or sometimes much worst, as seen in road rage.

Stitch is unable to reason or use rational thought while angry, instead of berating him and meeting anger with anger, try gentle tenderness (akahai).

When this happens you have a choice, either let him have the space and freedom to burn himself out, or you can respond with emotion, and the only emotion Stitch will respond to is aloha. The magic of aloha can be found in gentle tenderness and sprinkled in emotions such as love, kindness, empathy, and compassion. Stitch has to feel one of these from you, in order to escape the wave of emotional pain in which he is drowning.

Lilo will often comfort, cuddle, rock, and even sing to Stitch, to help calm him down (override the brains battle orientation). She endeavours to be patient, and pleasant, she understands that what he really needs is aloha (love) for you would not shout at a flower to make it grow.

Stitch is Lilo's pet therefore it is Lilo's (your human part of the mind) job to look after Stitch and stop it from getting into mischief, remember Stitch is your pet, and you need to teach it how to behave. Stitch is happy to learn new things, but Lilo must show that she loves Stitch, she must show kindness and compassion towards Stitch. Discover the trigger's, (the foods) that create the moods, the situations where Stitch feels overwhelmed, uneasy, stressed, or frightened, and have a collection of tools, and tricks, to calm, comfort and reassure. Explaining what is going to happen before it does happen can help, re-framing the experience, deescalating any stress build-up, distraction, and using entertainment techniques all work, the trick is anticipating an event and learning to use the right tool at the right time. Train Stitch to react in the way you want him to, and don't forget to reward any good behaviour.

As humans we naturally blame other people or our particular life script for making us angry, stressed, sad, or anxious, this is the Stitch part of our mind at work. In truth it's our own thoughts that dictate how we feel and determine our subsequent behaviour. We can always say to others, "I'm sorry Stitch (or any other name you wish to call him) got angry, but I've calm him down now."

Using the Stitch analogy above, we can learn to take responsibility for our actions and even change them. Open your mind, free your mind, and let innovative ideas flood your being.

Now let's move onto Nani:

Nani is Lilo's older sister, and she takes on the responsibility of protection, keeping the family (our body & being) away from danger. To do this she relies on her instinctive survival response mechanism, fight, flight, or freeze (Like in the film Bodyguard). In a perceived compromising situation, she will instantly choose one or more of those actions. Fight is to take on the threat; Flight is to run away from the threat; Freeze is to keep still and hope that the threat will go away, without noticing you. Nani will not always choose the right response because, it is made on her perception of the threat and how vulnerable she feels, which is simply based on instinct, and in turn is based on human survival, which is not always appropriate in modern-day society.

Remember when you ran away from the Banga boys, well that was the Nani part of your mind protecting you by opting to use the flight mode, and the Lilo part of your mind (the reasoning part) listening to Nani and taking the appropriate action, this is how it works. Sometimes though Lilo doesn't listen to Nani, and you might then find yourself in trouble.

In the past Polynesians would work on developing their sixth and seven sense, by using expanded sensory perception training techniques. And this is just what Nani (the fight or flight part of your mind) needs to do order to gain control of her feelings. Nani only has her innate sense of survival to guide her, she has no formal training, let me tell you a story.

On this island there is a very special tribe of ants, we can called them the 'rainbow ants' because they change colour depending on their sense of safety, their mood is reflected in their colour. When in the nest or resting they are white, when out and about but not stressed they are yellow, this could be classed as their normal everyday colour. But when they sense danger they warn each other by turning amber, and you see them readying themselves to engage in fight or flight. If the threat proceeds all the ants turn red and either run away as fast as they can, or immediately attack the threat. Nani could learn a lot by studying the rainbow ants.

Last but not least, we have Lilo:

Lilo is the thinking part of the mind, the part we identify as us, she is confident, considerate, and sensible, she bases her reactions on facts and logic. Lilo gathers facts and looks for the truth, she is open to suggestions and can reflect on them, she uses common sense with rational thinking. She takes responsibility for Stitch and when she loses control of her pet, she is old enough and mature enough, to recognise the disharmony caused and she will apologise for his actions.

As a seven-year-old Lilo is pre-programed with values and beliefs, based on her culture, religion, and education, one gained from family, friends and teachers, these beliefs became her filters, filters through which she will view the world, and interpret the information received by her senses. As she grows older, new personal life experiences will be added to her core beliefs, she will feel as though she has matured and has become an independent, confidant adult with her own beliefs.

The oceanic mind separates the junior from the adult.

At 20 years old, Lilo will be 7+13 in oceanic years, that's seven junior and thirteen senior years, at 30 she will be 7+23 that equates to seven years of beliefs that are not even hers, for she was a model, moulded by the motions, memories, and motivations of her mentors. The plus number represents her growth as an individual after the age of seven.

Understanding this is the key to becoming authentic, for the filters contained in the beliefs and prejudices obtained in your first seven years, can slow, or even block the flow of your authentic wave.

The question is what can you do about your filters?

Ka Huna Pono is the practice of becoming authentic, balanced, true to yourself, and in harmony with the environment. (Inner and outer environment)

The challenge is to develop the ability to:

- Change your thoughts. (Immediate action) – (Choose your wave – and change the brains chemistry)
- Change your filters. (Long term action) – (Learn to understand the ocean – and rewire the brain)

The aim is to improve your universal balance (pono) and to create harmony between your internal environment, and the external environment.

You are the creator of your own thoughts.

Your thoughts do not have the power to hurt you unless you give them that power. Remember thoughts are not real, they are your personalised, filtered, distortion of reality.

Lilo has the power to free the flow of her authentic wave. She might first start by learning to choose her mood, you don't have to ride the wave of emotions presented, let it pass, choose the wave you wish to ride, ask yourself, how do I want to feel, then adapt, create the feeling by focusing on thoughts that trigger the feeling. This will bring about immediate change to your chemistry, happy memories equals happy thoughts, happy thoughts equals happy chemicals, happy chemicals equals happy feelings, and happy feelings equals happy emotions. It's that simple but not that easy, just like learning to surf, practice, practice, practice.

Secondly by looking at Lilo's core beliefs, (those gained in her first seven years) she can pull them apart, reduce, and or remove the filters, rebuild new ones based on her own unique life experience, and enhanced insight gained by keeping an open mind, and an open heart.

To do this she should start by:

- Accept nothing, as true.
- Challenge perception
- Question everything

Challenge our perceptions, especially those gained while we were young, accept nothing as true until we have questioned and tested our beliefs. Kick out the old and bring in the new, design our own destiny, become authentic, embrace, and love the new you for being you, and no one else.

Mojo contemplated what he had just heard, his auntie loved quotes and he remembered she once quoted Socrates 'The unexamined life is not worth living.' Wow thought Mojo, just maybe, my mom is not always right after all, he loved this idea and vowed to challenge his own beliefs (and Moms) when he returns home, maybe auntie could help?

"Now you must go" said Maui, "you have a canoe to prepare."

The two of them flew out of the warriors ear, and instantly popped into full size Bees, Maui was grinning his biggest grin as he looked a Mojo, they both burst out laughing. And then, with a bish, bang, wallop, and a puff of smoke he was gone, the lights went out and everything was dark and silent.

Mojo was once again in his own body sitting in the cave lit by moon shadow, the only sound was the dark water swishing back and forth, he had a mixture of fear and excitement in his belly as he wondered.

What was about to happen...

Pele:

There was no time to lose, the air was black with volcanic dust, plumes of fire shot up into the heavens, the ground shook with thunderous applause. Mojo and Billy ran down to the canoe sitting at the water's edge, the golden sand had already turned black, Billy jumped onto the wooden deck and chewed through the rope anchoring it to a large rock, Mino was already clinging to the mask, he's not smiling now thought Mojo as he pushed the canoe out into the hot bubbling water, the lagoon was ablaze with burning ash, grabbing hold of his handmade paddle Mojo headed for the reef, the surf picked up and swept across the deck, Billy was glad he had climbed onto the box holding the coconuts, over the first wave, over the second wave, one more to go "hold tight" said Mojo out loud to no one in particular.

Bang!

The canoe had hit the reef, Mojo was hit by a barrelling wave with a mighty undertow, unable to get out of its path he was caught in the wash of the tumbling waves breaking on the reef. He was in real danger of being ripped apart on the sharp coral or being struck by the canoe, quietly he tried to stabilise a calm thought, one that had helped him ride out big, unsettling waves that sometimes hit without notice, keep clam, don't panic, breathe, and keep focused.

Then he felt a strong jerk...

As he found himself flying through the air, being towed by the canoe as it rode the crest of a wave high above the reef, and then skimming on the water's surface way beyond the reefs outer reaches, the loose flapping end of the rope had somehow wrapped itself around Mojo's leg, slamming him onto the wooden deck with a loud thud! Billy, Mino, and Mojo looked at each other and burst into laughter, "Wow what a ride" exclaimed Mojo.

Mojo glanced back and watched with his mouth wide open as the volcano spewed out lava, ash and hot rocks into the atmosphere "we need to leave" said Mojo "and quickly" within minutes the island was at the point of extinction, covered by a large black ash cloud, the water around them was being peppered by volcanic fire bombs thrown up into the sky by the blast, Mojo, Mino, and Billy, removed many of the coconuts and climbed into the wooden store box for protection, Bang! Bang! Bang! The rocks hit the canoe and the wooden box, that was lucky thought Mojo as he looked at the apocalyptic view through a gap in the timber.

Crack! It sounded like the earth had split apart, they were being sucked backwards towards the reef, faster and faster they travelled, then they were underwater and floating inside the box, next they were upright, and water was gushing out of the box. Feeling like rags in a washing machine Mojo, Mino and Billy clung onto each other for support.

All of a sudden Mojo noticed that they were yet again travelling away from the reef, they were surfing on top of the largest wave that he had ever seen at once he was in balance, in harmony, and in that moment he experienced infinity, a feeling of being one with the universe, and being embraced by creation itself.

Just then at the moment of pure stoke, he heard Moana's voice "don't be scared, we are from the ocean, it is our home, we are water people, who will end up back in the sea sooner or later."

In less than five minutes they found themselves miles away from the eruption, and completely outside of the danger zone, they looked back at where the island had been and marvelled at the firework display "awesome" shouted Mojo, "great fun" said Mino. Billy just stayed hidden inside the box with his head tucked under a few palm leaves.

Several hours and a few blisters later, Mojo and the crew of the makeshift canoe were taking stock, the black sky full of volcanic dust had merged with the darkness of the night, the only vision they had was supplied by a few glow worms that had somehow landed on the canoe. Mojo had bandaged his cut, using cloth from what was left of the burnt sail, chewed on coconut, and had drunk its milk. Now asked Mojo "how did this happen?"

Several weeks earlier he was sitting in the cave listening to Echo as the shell shared yet another Moana story, when the ground started to shake, at first with a gentle rhythmic vibration, the light streaming through the lava rock into the cave had red and amber hues, which mixed, danced, and flickered on the wet walls, as a scene of beauty appeared all around him. While watching intently he felt the presence of 'Pele' the spirit of the volcano, her ascending glory unfold before his eyes, this was a vision unlike any other, it felt like some sort of rip in the fabric of time, the water in the small pool inside the cave had been pulled apart and had raised itself into an impossible bubble, it then exploded into a wave, ran along the floor of the cave, over Mojo's legs and crashed against the opposite wall, before settling into the small crevice before repeating the movement all over again.

Moana's island of Motunui, was being destroyed by the extremely powerful, and unforgiving goddess Pele. She is acting just like Te Ka, the volcanic demon in her film. But why, what did we do? thought Mojo.

Then he heard a familiar voice in his head. That's right Mojo, just like the film, Maui started the disintegration of the goddess Te Fiti (mother earth) by stealing her heart, the heart of creation, he then gave her power to the human race. Sadly, as humans continue with their selfish ways of destruction, pollution, and over-population, the islands of the Pacific Ocean are drowning. It's not nature that needs fixing, it's our attitude to nature.

Te Fiti (mother earth) has the ability to look after herself, as she has always done. Like humans she also has an immune system, an extremely powerful immune system which has started to mount its own defence, a defence against the greatest threat to her survival: the human race.

We ourselves are beginning to be rejected by the planet, thought Mojo, and for the first time in history, human extinction is actually within striking distance. We need the earth much more than the earth needs us. We must be much more loving of our home, or we will end up homeless. -Scott Stillman

Mojo remembered the words of his kumu, "instead of just picking flowers for our leis, we should see ourselves as flowers that are part of the lei, we are not just a drop in the ocean, we are the complete ocean in a drop."

Only by returning the heart of creation was Maui able to save humanity, and only by returning to a creative loving, caring, and compassionate heart, can we save ourselves.

Wow! what was that! what had I just seen? Thought Mojo.

"That is tomorrows history yet to be made" said the soft gentle voice "be prepared or be overcome, you cannot change what's going to happen, but you can change how it affects you. We will all face what can appear to be an overwhelming level of devastation at some stage in our lives, how we choose to respond will define our next stage of development. Know that it's coming, be prepared, choose your response, then act, look to the rhythm of the tides."

The images disappeared as quickly as they had appeared, Mojo was full of questions, what did that mean? Was his first thought followed by, was it real? Could it be a message? All was quite around him as the cave returned back to normal. The experience left Mojo shaken, was this a vision of the future? If so I had better finish building the canoe and quickly, he thought to himself, what then followed, was weeks of frantic activity.

Mojo had been collecting materials to build a raft all summer, he had found a couple of coconut trees, ones that had fallen during the hurricane season, he had managed to roll the trunks down the beach by placing smaller broken branches from other trees onto the soft sand creating a kinda slipway, they now sat pride of place next to the water's edge. He had planned to use the branches as a deck, spanning the space between the two trunks, and lash them together with the string like bindings he had made from the leaves of the palm tree.

"Will it make the canoe sail better?" said a voice inside Mojo's head. He had collected several fallen palm trees, made rope from vine, shaped a rudder with wood salvaged from his destroyed boat, and made a sail from palm leaves. He had an image of a Polynesian canoe in his head and used that for the construction plan, now he had questions, lots of questions, how many coconuts do I take? Do I need to build a hut on the canoe? Do I need a second sail? Do I need a spare rudder? How do I know which way to sail? How much more time do I need to do all these things? Do I need to answer all these questions? He started to fill overwhelming stress build up, then he heard the voice again, "Canoes don't sink because of the water around them, they sink because of the water that gets in them. Don't let what's happening around you, get inside you and weight you down. Just ask yourself will it make the boat go better?"

Mojo remembered a book they had read at school about an Olympic rowing team, if they had a problem with the boat, the team would brainstorm the problem, come up with a load of ideas, which inevitably would led to a load more questions. All of which were filtered down to 'will it make the boat go better?' If the answer is yes, then the idea was kept, if the answer was no, then the idea was dumped. I'll do that thought Mojo.

Now I can plan my work then I can work my plan thought Mojo, it feels so much better to be organised and know what I must do.

As he toiled day and night his mind drifted back to a school lesson about a Polynesian voyaging canoe called 'Hokule'a (Star of Gladness) in the 1970's it looked like the one Moana and Maui had sailed in the D--n-y film. Well, the amazing thing was is that they didn't use a single nail, every part was lashed together using miles of rope, Mojo was now doing the same weaving together the past and present.

Mojo was lost in thought, his project to rescue the future was totally focusing his mind on the job at hand, time seamed to fly, and the work became effortless, there was no space for self-pity, anxiety or worry, as another length of wood was lashed onto the newly assembled raft, looking good thought

Mojo as it took shape, each piece of the puzzle being added bit by bit. Moana and Maui would be proud of me, I'm proud of me, thought Mojo with a big grin on his face.

Just then Billy brushed up against Mojo, laid down and rested his head on Mojo's lap, instantly returning him back to the canoe and the reality of the present moment. "You know Billy, I'm really happy that you and Mino are here with me, as we ride this canoe on the high seas of life" with a smile on his face and a heart full of gratitude, Mojo said, "Mahalo Moana, thank you for the vision, thank you for sharing your story, thank you for letting me experience the magic of your island cave, and for Echo the shell of sounds, it will live with me forever, I promise to live the aloha way and follow the path that has given me guidance for without it we would have been rudderless".

We will forever remain spiritually bonded thought Mojo as he drifted into the world of dreams, feeling happy and contented, he floated on the currents hoping to find a safe island and a new tomorrow."

'You're welcome, go splash, be joyful, have fun, be kind' come the soft gentle reply.

Note from Mojo:

On his return Mojo wrote the following note which he reads and acts upon everyday:

1. Go Splash
2. Be Joyful
3. Have Fun
4. Be Kind

Next to the words he placed the following guidance:

1. **Go Splash**
   Go make a Splash~ engage in Sport; Play; Leisure; Art; and you are on your way, add both socializing and helping and you have a winning formula.

2. **Be Joyful**
   Share the joy, bring enthusiasm to all that you do, it will help make you and others to feel better. Be interested and be interesting.

3. **Have Fun**
   Don't take life too seriously, look on the bright side of life, have fun, laugh a lot, especially at yourself.

4. **Be Kind**
   Find a way to help someone every day. (Preferably someone you don't know) Change the way people feel for the better, put a smile on someone's face, do random acts of kindness.

   Daily mantra.......... "Go Splash a little joy, have fun, be kind."

GO SPLASH:

Go Splash!! Is an interactive formula that promotes a joyful mindset, leading to positive mental health and well-being.

Surfing Waves of Aloha has a harmonising effect on both mind and body, it is a soulful practice, full of joy, love, and laughter.

Good vibrations flood the body and changes the way people feel for the better.

Go Splash, consist of six evidenced based actions aimed at improving personal well-being and mental health.

The word 'splash' is split into two groups, the first four letters and the last two. The aim is to take one action out of the first group and to couple it, with one action from the second group, this will kick-start the process. If you add a second action from group two, then the magic really begins.

1. **Sport:** Being active and engaged in exercise can help you feel better, physically, and mentally. Sport helps you focus on the moment and leaves your stress behind.
2. **Play:** Smile, be cheerful, have fun, laugh a lot, and let the child inside you run loose.
3. **Leisure:** Take time to appreciate nature, go for a walk in a green space, park, or woodlands. Enjoy natures blue space, by

a lake or on the beach, go for a swim. Listen to music, get involved in cooking or gardening. Walk slowly and you will go far.

4. **Art:** Do what you love doing, take time to enjoy being in the moment, get lost in your art and time will fly. Being present and focused on the moment directly enhances your well-being.
5. ....
6. **Socialising:** Friends are the best medicine, share stories with friends, family, or your preferred social group. Do not stay isolated and on your own for too long, mixing with and being valued by others is a fundamental human need.
7. **Helping:** This is all about giving your time, not money. A single act of kindness each day can increase your well-being. People who help others are more likely to rate themselves as feeling happy.

Sport & physical activity can have a positive impact on our body and mind and help both our mental and physical health. It can.....

- Help us cope with the stress of daily life more effectively.
- Help us build confidence and self-esteem.
- Reduce symptoms of depression and anxiety.
- Give us a natural energy boost.
- Help us maintain a healthy weight.
- Improve our physical strength.
- Help us meet new people and make friends.
- Improve concentration and sleeping patterns.
- Improve our mood. (When we exercise our body releases chemicals that make us feel happy, it produces happy waves).

Go Splash~ Tools, Tips, Tricks, & Triggers:

- Go Splash is a proactive, integrated mind-body practice for positive mental health and wellbeing.
- To change the way you feel, you have to change your emotional state. Here we offer you some tools, tips, and tricks to trigger that change.
- Research shows that keeping a journal can help us gain control of our emotions, and improve our mental health, because it is an effective way of expressing things in a more structured and organised way.

It offers us a way to understand symptoms and improve our mood by:

- Helping us prioritise problems, fears, and concerns.
- Tracking thoughts, feelings, and symptoms to identify triggers and learn ways to better control them.
- Providing us an opportunity to focus on the positive and identifying negative thoughts and behaviour.

When we are feeling stressed its often difficult to think clearly, so recording it (drawing or writing it down) can help to identify what's causing the problem, stress, or anxiety. Once we have managed to identify the problem, it can then be easier to resolve, and help us reduce our stress levels.

Go with the flow. There is no wrong way to do this, pick a page that appeals to you and just write or draw whatever feels right. You can work with one or more pages at a time, it's up to you, you decide.

Just like playing sport or any physical activity, you're doing something beneficial for your mind. The tools, tips and tricks on the following pages offer some structure and a suggested starting point.

Fill me in:

My name is..

I enjoy doing: (list the things you enjoy doing)

I would like to do: (list the things you would like to try)- Trying new things can be scary as it takes us out of our comfort zone, but often the things we fear don't actually happen. Trying something new can also give us a profound sense of achievement.

Being active makes me feel: (Write or draw how you feel)

What is going well for me? (Every time something goes well, write it down along with how it makes you feel)

When I'm with my friends I feel: (Talking, spending time, and being valued by others is a fundamental human need)

Today I am grateful for: (write down one or two things that you are grateful for today)

What makes me feel good: (write down what makes you feel good etc- music, pets, playing)

What makes me feel proud: (What have you achieved of which you are really proud? Close eyes and focus on how you feel when you are really proud)

My playlist: (write a list of songs that make you feel happy – play and singalong when you want to be happy)

What makes me feel better: (Sport, play, leisure, art, socialising and helping can make us feel better mentally and physically- fill out the list below)

Activity: How does my mind and body feel?

GO SPLASH!!

How do I feel in nature: (Green & Blue is calling you. Being in nature can make us feel better mentally and physically- fill out the list below)

Place: How does my body and mind feel?

Park

Woods

Field

Farm

Swimming Pool

Sea

In the Rain

Beach

Add your own place here.

Being organised:

Being organised has lots of benefits. It can help us on specific task, it can free up time and energy, help improve sleep, reduce stress levels and some symptoms of depression and anxiety.

Have a think about your life and whether you would like it to be more organised. Try to do this when you are feeling calm, rather than when you might be feeling anxious or uneasy.

Plan your work (your day) work your plan. List your things to do today and put them in order of priority.

What makes me feel excited: (How do you feel when you are excited?)

O'Hana: (O'hana is family and anyone you treat as family.)

Name of person: When I'm with this person I feel:

Magic Moments: (Take time to enjoy the moment and the environment around you, savouring the moment enhances your well-being etc: today I saw some ducklings, spring flowers, Mum gave me a hug)

Keep Learning: (What would I like to learn? Learning new things can have a positive effect on self-esteem and self-worth)

Helping others: (Doing an act of kindness once a day has been found to increase your well-being and happiness levels)

I am learning to be successful: (You only fail if you give up. Until then there is no such thing as failure, only lessons and practice. Practice what you learn and learn from your practice)

My promise to me: (List the things that you are going to do in order to make you feel better. Then celebrate by doing something special every time you complete a promise)

I'm going to improve my physical wellness by doing:-

I'm going to improve my mental wellness by doing:-

Sleeping habits:

A lack of sleep can have a negative impact on our mental health, conversely mental health problems such as stress can affect our sleep.

Here are some tips and tricks to gaining better sleep.

- Try to go to bed at the same time each night and get up at the same time each morning.
- If you can, avoid sleeping in – try to maintain a routine.
- If you need a nap, aim for 20 minutes; this is enough to feel rested and ready to get on with your day.
- Spend time outside during the day to get as much exposure to natural light as possible.
- If possible, avoid screens before bed – the blue light emitted from devices interferes with your ability to sleep.
- Take time to wind down before you go to bed: have a warm bath, read, listen to relaxing music.
- Ensure your bedroom is cool, dark, and quite; consider using ear plugs if you find noise disturbs you.
- Make sure you have eaten and drunk enough during the day so that hunger and thirst don't wake you up in the night.

    (Sport In Mind)

Art of Aloha: (Notes or drawings ~ add your personal art here)

A Day at the Beach:

An invite 4U:

Mojo spent many months on the beach, he made friends, had lots of fun and many adventures. He listened to Moana's story's about her childhood and growing up, he also learned a lot about himself as he shared happy days at her surf n' sand school.

This book shares some of his beach day experiences, but there are many more still untold. If you can imagine an adventure that Mojo might have had during one single day at the beach, we invite you to share your story: Write a one or two page story about a day at the beach for Mojo and email it along with your name and age to *abigsplash4u@gmail.com* the best ones will be included into the next addition of this book.

The Big Splash!!

If this book has helped you just a little bit, join the big splash, pay forward, gift a copy to someone you know, and help change the way they feel, for the better.

The more books we drop into the sea of community support, the bigger the splash (of positive mental health & wellbeing) the stronger the wave, and the more people are reached by the ripple effect of all our efforts.

All profits (100%) are used to support Surf & Beach Therapy communities ....this is Aloha in Action.

Afterword:

There are two fish swimming through the coral reef on a nice sunny morning, they pass an old crab resting on the sand, he smiles at them and says, "morning boys, how's the water?" The two fish nod back and swim on for a while, then eventually one of them looks over at the other and goes, "what the hell is water?"

The aim and inspiration for this book is to inform, educate and entertain through simple awareness.

Awareness of what is so real and essential, so hidden in plain sight, all around us, all the time, that we have to keep reminding ourselves over and over: This is water. -David Foster Wallace

How do the two fish relate to us.

As humans we live our lives in an ocean of emotion, every second of everyday we are hit by waves of thoughts and feelings, they affect every element of our being.

You can't stop mind waves, but you can learn to surf them.

Surf therapy is not just about learning to surf waves of water, it's about discovering the unbridled joy, fun and laughter of playing in the surf, gaining confidence and self-belief, then using the experience to change the chemistry of the brain, so that you can develop the skills to surf waves of thoughts, feelings, and emotions.

Surf Therapy is an immersive bodymind experience..........

"When you're surfing, you're not thinking about what's waiting for you on land. That presence, that ability to be in the zone, to connect to yourself, it changes the way you see the world and changes how you relate to others. The ocean heals you, humbles you, and is all-inclusive – it is truly the great equalizer." - Kris Primacio ISTO CEO

Oceanic Heritage:

Hawaiians are losing their land, and their culture is being taken away from them by western society. Surfing, Hula, and Lomilomi was practiced by Hawaiian royalty, it is the last bastion of nobility, and by claiming ownership for themselves western society are being disrespectful to the whole Polynesian culture.

Aloha is the art of giving without expecting anything in return, and the azura community support initiative have been engaged in living the 'aloha in action concept.'

By acknowledging and practicing the living 'Art of Aloha' through massage therapy, surf therapy and beach activities, while supporting and highlighting the legitimate sovereignty of the pacific island people, azura hope to take one small step towards honouring the ancestors and bringing the rightful recognition back to the people of Hawaii and Oceania.

Ua ma uke o ka 'aina ka pono ~ the life of the land is perpetuated in righteousness.

Mahalo Nui

About the Author:

Kevin is a Grandude, Chiropractor, and Sports therapist who has been engaged in voluntary service since 1968, using his knowledge and skills on sports fields, in clinics and rehab centres, workshops, presentations, demonstrations, and publications, to help improve people's mental health and physical wellbeing.

He has spent over 50 years collaborating closely with athletes presenting with physical injuries and associated mental health stress.

He co-developed the 'living aloha' concept from which the azura 'aloha in action' project was born, this self-funded initiative has been inspiring and supporting healing artist since its inception in 1984 and subsequently formulated into the 'Go Splash' mantra for everyday living.

This book is the latest in the trilogy celebrating the outreach programs of the azura project, the inspiration as always is to inform, educate and entertain.

He is not only a lifelong community volunteer, but one who always gives more when things get tough.

During Covid lockdown as his business slowed and stopped, Kevin became a volunteer vaccinator working with St. Johns ambulance, activity participating in their efforts to vaccinate the people of the UK.

Although he is now in his sixties and adapting to arthritis, he can still be found on a beach assisting, surf therapy, and helping sport organisations to improve, and change the lives of people, young and old.

"Time is a gift you give to others. To live with aloha is to give for the pleasure of giving, without expecting anything in return" – Kevin England DC. DD.

Living Aloha:

This is my story formulated from my life experience, imagination, and mindful practice.

I have adopted a joyously free-form personal philosophy, a free-flow of spiritual energy in which our identity is seen as a momentary embodiment of the ongoing stream of life.

I am interested in the aloha spirit and the evolution of consciousness.

I am here visiting for a while.

I am a spirit being, here to have the human experience.

I am energy embodied in human form.

I surf waves of thoughts and feelings.

I smile and look for the beauty in all life.

I have an infinite aspect to myself.

I am part of the universal whole.

I will return to the matrix of universal consciousness.

My personal philosophy is not pure science, it is not pure theology, and it is not pure metaphysics. It is something else, something different, something betwixt and between, what is and what could be.

I am trying to redefine my spirituality in terms that make sense to me and for our times.

Flow is a source of physic energy in that it focuses attention and motivates action. The free flow of this loving, joyful energy, learning to use it well, in harmony and in balance with the environment, is the essence of life ~ too ride Waves of Aloha.

I speak metaphorically, using approximations to underly the reality that I believe in, but cannot express adequately.

I know that my knowledge is itself evolving, and through that evolution in a few years will have to be expressed in entirely different terms.

But it all kind of hangs together quite easily for me. It may sound flippant, but the thing is 'Living Aloha' is a practice of spiritual expansion.

Aloha is my art and a gift to be shared.............

(Adapted from I am)

Bibliography:

Bleakley. S. (2016). **Mindfulness and Surfing.** UK: Leaping Hare.

Borg. J. (2010). **Mind power.** UK: Pearson Education.

Chang. B. (2006). **Riding Quantum Waves.** USA: Destiny Tech Press.

Chernoff. M&A.(2021). **Getting Back to Happy.** USA. Penguin Random House.

Chiles. W. (1995). **Secrets & Mysteries of Hawaii.** USA: Health Communications.

Coleman. S. (2001). **Eddie Would Go.** USA: Mind Raising Press.

Csikszentmihalyi. M. (1997). **Finding Flow.** USA: Perseus Books.

Davis. D. (2015). **Waterman.** USA: University of Nebraska Press.

Dyer. W. (2007). **Change Your Thoughts Change Your Life**. UK: Hay House.

England. K. (2012). **Starlite Lomi.** UK: Panoma Press.

England. K. (2015). **Stardance.** UK: Panoma Press.

Gately. I. (2018). **The Secret Surfer.** UK: Apollo Books.

Gore. A. & Lewis. L. (2015). **Joy is an Inside Job.** Australia: Head2Head.

Jim. H.U. (2007). **Wise Secrets of Aloha.** USA: Weiser Books.

King. S.J. (2008). **Huna.** USA: Atria Books.

Kotler. S. (2021). **Art of the Impossible.** USA: Harper Wave.

Lambert. C. (2019). **Waves of Healing.** USA: Heather Leigh Press.

Nichols. W. (2014). **Blue Mind.** USA: Abacus.

O'Dell. S. (1960). **Island of the Blue Dolphins.** USA: Yearling Books.

O'Reilly. D. (2020). **Surfing the Waves of Stress.** UK. Amazon.

Pearsall. P. (1996). **Pleasure Prescription.** USA: Hunter House.

Rios. C. (2000). **Ka Hana Pono.** Hawaii: Hilo Bay.

Smith. R. (2008). **Awakening the Energy Body.** USA: Bear & Co.

Stillman. A. (2022). **Oceans of my Mind.** USA: Wild Soul Press.*

Thompson. H. (2018). **One Wave at a Time.** USA: Whitman & Co.

Yogis. J. (2009). **Saltwater Buddha.** USA: Wisdom Publications.

Yogis. J. (2017). **All our Waves are Water.** USA: Harper wave.

Milton Keynes UK
Ingram Content Group UK Ltd.
UKHW040137170224
437973UK00001B/91